G000090092

People at Work

Working for a Garage

by Graham Rickard

Photography by Tim Humphrey

Titles in the series

Working at an Airport
Working in the Army
Working for a Brewery
Working on a Building Site
Working for a Bus Company
Working for a Chemicals Company
Working for the Civil Service
Working at a Coal Mine
Working at a Port
Working in a Department Store
Working for an Electronics Company
Working on a Farm
Working for a Food Company
Working at a Garage
Working in a Hospital
Working in a Hotel
Working for an Insurance Company
Working at a Light Engineering Plant
Working on a Newspaper
Working for an Oil Company
Working for the Police Force
Working in a Town Hall
Working for Yourself

First published in 1984 by
Wayland (Publishers) Ltd
49 Lansdowne Place, Hove
East Sussex BN3 1HF, England

ISBN 0 85078 412 3

Phototypeset by Kalligraphics Ltd,
Redhill, Surrey
Printed and bound in Great Britain by
R. J. Acford Ltd, Industrial Estate, Chichester, Sussex

Contents

The Motor Trade Today 6
Dutton-Forshaw's Garage, Preston 8

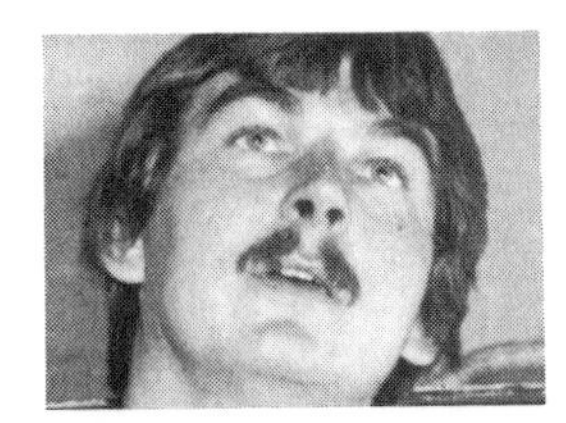

Ian Wilson
Mechanic
10

Steve Geldert
Counter Partsman
15

Carol Gillybrand
Van Driver
20

Iqbal Patel
Body Repairer
24

Andrew Cross
Youth Training Scheme Trainee
29

Nicola Todd
Trimmer
34

Gary Bretherton
Foreman, Rolls-Royce Service Section
39

Jackie Davis
Parts/Costing Clerk
44

Ian Brown
Service Manager
49

Alan Barnard
Service Receptionist
54

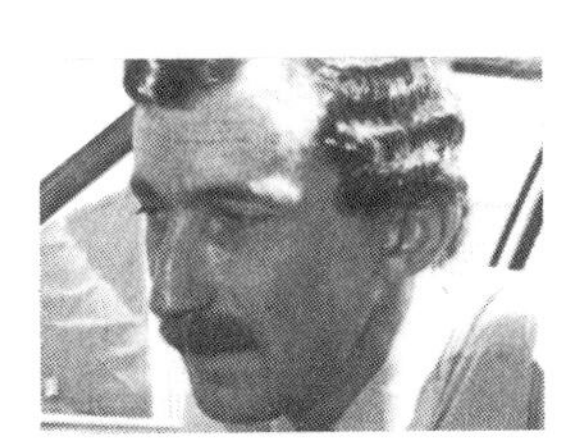

Hugh Duckworth
Sales Manager
58

David Lyon
Managing Director
63

Jobs in a Garage 68
Sources of Further Information 68
Index 69

The Motor Trade Today

In 1896, the American, Henry Ford produced his 'Model T', the first mass-production car, and started one of the world's biggest industries. Manufacturers in other countries opened factories and soon almost everyone seemed to want to own a car. This, in turn, gave birth to other industries; selling, repairing and servicing cars, and supplying petrol to run them, soon became big business. Today, Britain's motor trade is the country's third largest industry; 450,000 people are employed in garages – even more than those who work in the factories which make the cars. In financial terms, the car distribution system in the UK is the country's largest distribution system of consumer durables (items which do not require frequent replacement, i.e. because they are durable). Apart from a house, a car is the largest single purchase which anyone is likely to make, and it is usually a purchase which is repeated every few years.

Thirty-three manufacturers supply the British market, and in 1982 they sold over 1.5 million new cars, worth £7 billion. The trade also sold 2 million used cars in that year, and about the same number were probably sold privately.

As well as selling cars, most garages are involved in other aspects of the motor trade, all of which offer employment opportunities. Their repair and service workshops employ mechanics, auto-electricians and body repairers. Training for these jobs traditionally consisted of an apprenticeship for several years, including specialist college courses and direct work experience on the shopfloor. No reasonably-sized garage can function efficiently without a well-stocked spare-parts store run by a fully-trained team, to supply both the mechanics and the public with the parts which they need. Garage forecourts are no longer restricted to just selling petrol; they now supply a wide range of items, including tyres, batteries, lubricants and accessories. Garages also employ reception staff, costing clerks, secretaries and various other types of personnel.

However, the retail motor industry is going through a very tough time, despite a current sales boom. Ten per cent of the members of the Motor Agents Association went out of business in 1982, and over the last few years the number of people involved in the motor trade has been drastically reduced. More than half the cars sold in Britain are now imported from Europe and Japan, and demand has fallen over the last ten years. Because manufacturing capacity now far exceeds the market demand, fierce competition between manufacturers has led to decreased profit margins for the suppliers. Many businesses could not increase turnover to make up for the drop in profits, and this has led to redundancies and liquidations.

The new generation of cars need much less servicing because of their advanced design and the increased use of electronics. In the short term this has led to a fall in the need for workshop staff, particularly in the area of routine servicing. While this will probably mean that garages may not need as many all-round skilled mechanics, there will be a requirement for more specialist staff to cover such work as automatic transmissions, computerized electrical equipment and air conditioning. Most garages have now broken with the traditional fixed period of apprenticeship and are now looking at a different form of

Henry Ford's Model T cars coming off the production line, in the 1890s.

More than half the cars sold in Britain are imported. These Volkswagon Golfs at the Volkswagon factory in Germany are ready for distribution.

traineeship, designed to meet the needs of a more sophisticated industry.

A new development is the Youth Training Scheme, which is intended to help school-leavers and unemployed young people in the transition from school to working life. It will hopefully give employers a better-trained and more highly motivated workforce.

In the motor industry, the Scheme is managed by national companies such as the Dutton-Forshaw Motor Group. Smaller garages assist in this by offering 'on the job' training to young people. The Scheme gives work experience in the trades of vehicle mechanics, body repairers, painters, partsmen, and clerk/administrators. 'Off the job' training, lasting thirteen weeks, is, in most cases, carried out at a college of further education. However, some companies set up their own training workshops for this purpose. The year's course leads to the relevant Part 1 City and Guilds examination. At the end of the year trainees who are not offered a job with their sponsor company will, hopefully, be better equipped to find a job elsewhere.

With increased competition and lower profits, the motor trade is likely to face drastic changes over the next few years, with fewer garages operating. Those who survive will need high quality, well-motivated staff, to give the best possible standards of service to the public.

The motor trade is Britain's third largest industry, employing thousands of people.

Dutton-Forshaw's Garage, Preston

Dutton-Forshaw is a national company, run from its head office in Preston. The company is a subsidiary of SUITS (Scottish Universal Investment Trusts) which in turn is part of Lonrho, the giant international company with worldwide interests in almost every sphere of commerce and industry. The Dutton-Forshaw Motor Group is divided into four regions, each under its own managing director. The Preston branch is the largest of the company's six garages in the North West region, employing 110 of the 350 total work-force in the region. The garage sells over one-third of the company's regional sales of 5,000 new cars a year, as well as another 1,000 used cars. In fact, the garage is one of the North West's largest distributors and retailers of cars and spare parts, supplying many other garages in the region.

The regional group sells only British-made cars, and for many years has held franchises

A serviced car is delivered to the main entrance of Dutton-Forshaw, ready to be driven away by its owner.

from BL and Rolls-Royce to sell and distribute their cars exclusively. Rolls-Royce and Jaguar in particular, expect very high standards in sales and service from their franchised dealers; these standards are constantly reviewed, and Dutton-Forshaw has a high reputation to maintain.

The business in the North West was originally called Loxhams garages, and was started by Ewart Bradshaw, the founder of the motor trade in Preston. He began as a bicycle dealer at the beginning of the century, and then started selling cars. The name Loxhams Garages remained until 1969, when the business was taken over by the Dutton-Forshaw Motor Group, who were themselves taken over by SUITS, in 1980.

The garage now has a large modern showroom filled with Austin-Rover, Jaguar, and Rolls-Royce cars. The service and repair workshop is large and well-equipped with the latest plant and electronic equipment, and the parts department carries an enormous computerized stock of spares. The company is also involved in contract hire and fleet sales to large companies and public authorities. The body shop is separate from the mechanical workshop, and employs a number of panel-beaters and paint sprayers.

Dutton-Forshaw used to take on several apprentices every year, to be trained as mechanics, body repairers and other skilled craftsmen, to ensure a steady supply of highly-trained workers in their garages. But with higher costs and a contraction in business, the fixed period apprenticeship may soon become a thing of the past. To help fill the gap, and to reduce the numbers of young unemployed people, Dutton-Forshaw are playing a very active role as managing agents in the Government's new Youth Training Scheme.

This year the personnel manager for the

In the repair workshop, mechanics discuss the problem of an engine replacement with the service manager.

North West interviewed about 150 school-leavers, and accepted 110 as trainees. The trainees are sent to garages both inside and outside the motor group headquarters, for practical experience and formal training, including one day per week at the training centre at Dutton-Forshaw, Preston. The training only lasts one year, but should provide trainees with a sound basic foundation in their chosen craft, which will stand them in good stead when they come to look for a permanent job. As a managing agent for the Scheme, Dutton-Forshaw are in a unique position in the North West, and the company hopes that its efforts will help both school-leavers and the industry, by ensuring a steady flow of skilled labour.

Below *The computerized parts department carries an enormous stock of spares.*

Ian Wilson

Mechanic

Ian Wilson first gained mechanical experience in his father's motorbike business. He joined Dutton-Forshaw seven years ago, and now works as a mechanic in the car servicing workshop.

I left school when I was fifteen with no qualifications at all. It was a local secondary modern school, about three miles from Preston, and I left without even sitting any CSE or 'O' level exams. But I already had plenty of mechanical experience because my dad had a motorbike business, and I had been helping him since I was about seven years old. I was always interested in bikes and engines, and every night, after school, I used to work in my dad's shop.

When I left school I worked full-time for my dad, with my two brothers and two mechanics. When we had enough experience, we took over from the mechanics, and did all the work between us – it was a real family business. It went well to start with, but after six years the business went downhill, and we had less and less work. The area also deteriorated to the point where it more or less became a slum, and in the end my dad was forced to close down the business.

I was twenty-one at the time, and decided to try my hand at something new. A friend of mine in the road transport business had a broken-down lorry, and I agreed to mend it for him. In return, he paid for me to be trained to drive heavy goods vehicles, and I passed my HGV Class 1 driving test. I worked for him for about a year, but it wasn't really a success, so I decided to give up lorry-driving and go back to being a mechanic.

In the jobcentre I saw that Dutton-Forshaw were advertising for a mechanic, so I rang them immediately, and arranged an interview with the service manager. At the interview, he wanted to know how long it took me to change a gearbox, how long I had worked for previous employers, why I had left them, and several other questions about my practical skills and experience. He agreed to take me on a month's trial, and I started on the following Monday.

That was seven years ago, and I'm still here. I think they kept me on because I'm pretty good at my job, I'm never late, and I don't take days off. I'm honest, I work hard, and I'll have a go at any job, no matter what it may involve.

I was very pleased to get the job; it was just what I wanted, and the first few days here were really good. I remember being very impressed by the size of the workshop, and all its facilities – the ramps, pits and special tools. I got on well with my workmates, and everything seemed to be done very efficiently, compared with the other places I had worked in.

At first I worked on Rover and Triumph cars, repairing and servicing them. To improve my practical and theoretical training, the company sent me on several day-release and weekly courses, and I took a Ministry of Transport course which qualifies me to test vehicles and issue their annual MOT certificates. Whenever BL produce a new car or engine, they have training courses for mechanics, and I go to those as well.

I can turn my hand to just about anything in the workshop, but most of the time I work on a modern car-servicing flowline system introduced recently by BL. It's called 'Leycare' and is a very fast and efficient way of doing routine services. There are only two of us working on it, but on a good day we can get through seventeen complete services a day. We have our own separate bay in the workshop, our own special tools, and a large collection of routine spare parts immediately to hand. With the new Leycare system, we can test everything on the service sheet – brakes, lights, steering, the lot. We have special electronic equipment for analysing the engine's performance. It's a very efficient way of spotting problems on a car, and if we find any major faults, we hand the car over to the workshop to be fixed and move on to the next

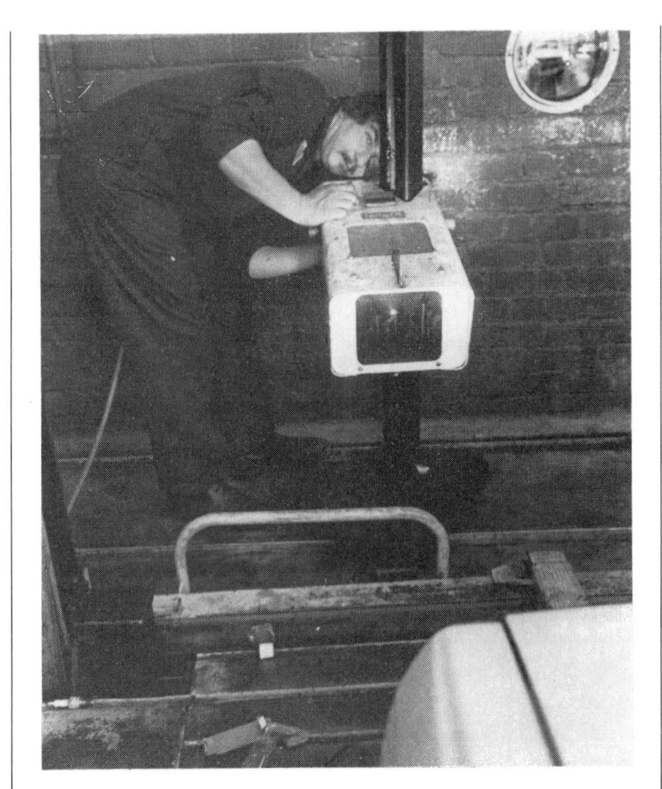

Ian is testing and aligning the beams of a car's headlights.

Ian stands in the inspection pit to drain the used oil out of the engine sump.

Checking the tyre pressures.

The service area has its own stock cupboard, from which Ian gets all the materials necessary to service a car.

one. We used to take it in turns to work on the Leycare servicing, but now I work on it permanently. The company is sending me on a BL Leycare course soon, so hopefully we'll get even more efficient on these routine services.

We don't officially start work until 8.45 a.m. but I usually start as soon as I arrive, just after 8.00 a.m. I open up the tools and spares cupboards. We then finish off any work left over from the night before, and do the day's paperwork. As well as filling out service sheets for each car, we have to order spares, and keep a careful record of the time spent on each car and the spares that we've used, so that the customer will get an accurate bill. My wife works out the bills for a lot of the work that I do, because she works in the office as a costing clerk.

We have service sheets which cover every make of car, showing lubrication points, correct gaps on spark plugs and all the information we need to do a complete service. To get through each day's work, we have to work fast, but we also have to be careful, and check everything thoroughly to make sure that we don't miss any faults. Most of the cars are in the Austin-Rover range, but we have to be able to service any car which a customer brings in. I hate leaving a job half-finished, so I always complete the service I'm working on before my wife and I go home to lunch at about 12.30 p.m.

In the afternoon we carry on working until we have finished all the services for the day. If a customer brings in his car for servicing in the morning, he expects to have it back that evening, so it's important to have all the work finished on time. We use several special tools to do the service work, including Krypton electronic tuning for the engine, brake testers, headlamp-beam setters and tracking gauges to align the wheels. I also have my own set of 'Snap-On' tools which I keep in a metal tool-

He checks the information book for the correct engine settings of a BL car.

chest. I buy them from a rep who regularly visits the garage – they're very good, but certainly not cheap – mine are insured for £1,000.

If we finish our work early, I usually go and help out somewhere else in the workshop. If someone has half-finished a job, and given it up because they're having problems, I like to tackle it and sort it out – for me, a problem is a challenge. If a customer brings in a very 'sick' car, and we do a good job on it and give it back to him working perfectly, then I feel that I share in his satisfaction. It also gives the garage a good reputation, and generates more work for us all in the future.

Sometimes it's a bit of a headache keeping our parts store well-stocked. It's difficult to keep a stock of everything when you're working on every make of car. Sometimes, when we run out of something, I queue at the main stores, only to find that they don't have the parts I need either – that can be frustrating because it holds everything up.

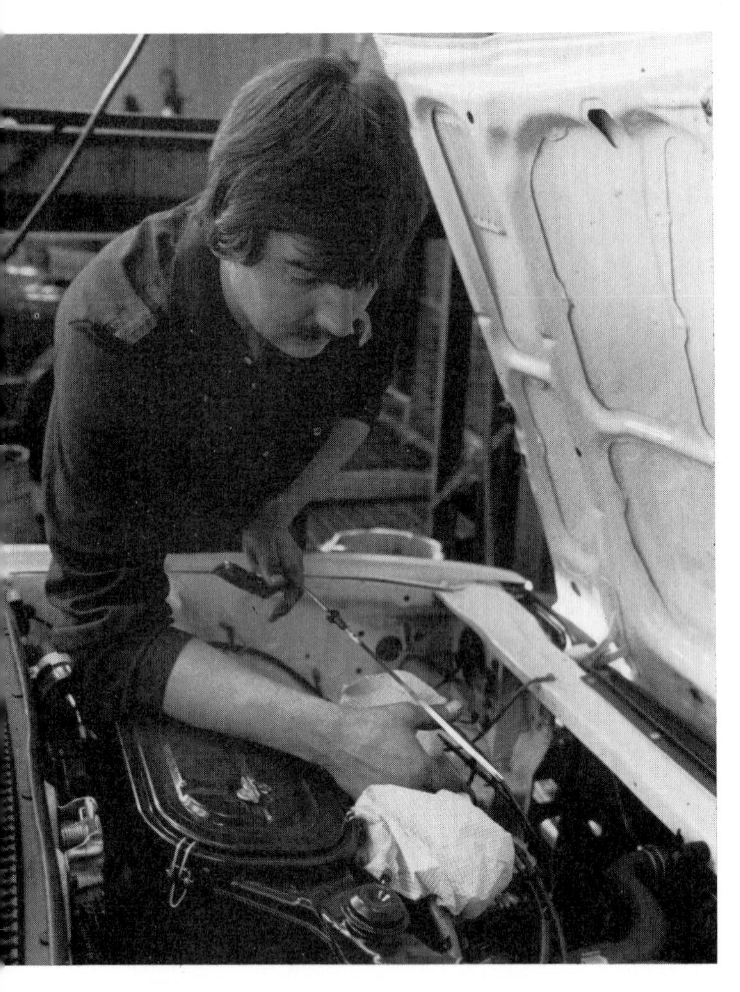

Checking the oil level in the engine sump, before service completion.

Ian re-times a car with the aid of a 'timing gun'.

It's a good place to work though, and I enjoy my job. I get on well with my mates and the bosses, and there's a good working atmosphere here. The money's good too, if you work hard, because we're on a bonus system – the more services we get through, the more we earn. There's no chance of hiding my pay-packet from my wife, though, because she's the one who works out my pay!

This workshop isn't unionized, but, on my dad's advice, I joined the AUEW (Amalgamated Union of Engineering Workers) when I first left school, and I've been a member ever since. Every six months I go to the local union office to pay my membership of 30p a week. The union would help me if I ever had problems at work, but also many workshops are 'closed shops' and would never employ me unless I was a member.

I get the usual staff discounts from the garage, but apart from that I don't get any perks in my job. Although I like my job, I'd like to think I'll get promoted one day. I don't want to spend the rest of my life doing car services, but there are so many people here more qualified than I am that I think my chances are pretty slim. If the Leycare servicing section expands, the company might decide to employ a Leycare supervisor, and that could be my chance of promotion.

When I'm not working, cars still take up most of my time, and are my main interest in life. I have my own Triumph Dolomite, and most weekends are taken up with working on that, or on friends' cars – I just don't seem to get much time for any other interests. My wife and I would like to go abroad for a holiday, but we haven't yet managed to do so. I would like to go to Australia, to see if I like the place. Then I wouldn't mind emigrating out there; it would mean living in a better climate, with higher wages and more opportunities, and it would be a complete change.

Steve Geldert

Counter Partsman

Steve Geldert started work in the parts department at Dutton-Forshaw soon after leaving school. He has to know about the thousands of different motor parts and he uses a computer to keep track of them all.

My father is a plasterer and my mum works in a factory, so I didn't grow up in the motor trade, and I had no real interest in it until I got this job. I went to a Catholic comprehensive school here in Preston, which I left when I was sixteen, with eight CSEs, including maths, accounts, and commerce. I had no real idea of what I wanted to do when I left school, so I worked with my dad for a couple of months as a plasterer's labourer. I decided that I liked the work, and tried to get a plasterer's apprenticeship, but I was too late. Most places had already been filled, and I couldn't get anyone to take me on.

My brother works here in the parts department of Dutton-Forshaw, and after talking to him about his job, I liked the sound of it and thought I'd have a try at it myself. There were no jobs advertised, but I just went ahead and wrote to six local garages. About two weeks later, I had replies from two garages (this was one of them) asking me to come for an interview. The first time Dutton-Forshaw just gave me an aptitude test – it was fairly simple, but I had to be quick.

About a week later I had the real interview, which was mainly a test of my knowledge of vehicles. The parts manager had several car components on the desk in front of him, and when he asked me what they were, I didn't know a single one! I didn't think I stood a chance after that, but he asked me other questions about my school, my background and my interests. I didn't know my exam results at the time, and he wanted to know if I would be willing to re-take them if I failed, because most people in this job do have several CSEs.

I had a third informal interview which my parents were invited to, and the parts manager and general manager told me what was involved in the job and showed me around the building. I was really pleased when I was

Steve uses a microfiche to locate the coding numbers of spares.

Checking the parts and the code numbers before despatching goods to customers.

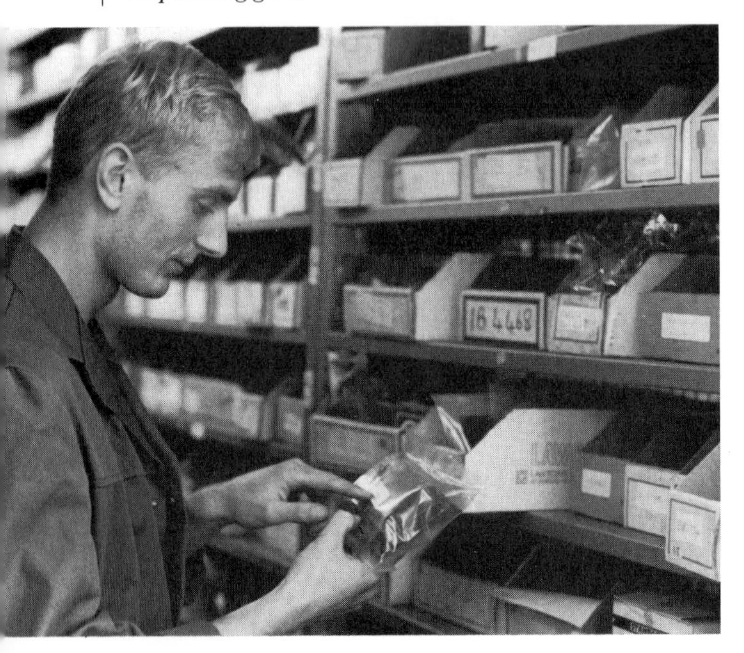

offered the job, about a week later. I think I did well in the aptitude test, and in spite of my ignorance of car parts, I showed more interest in the work than the other applicants. I was told later that they were pleased with my exam results, and thought I would learn the job quickly.

I did very simple work to start with, just putting parts in the right place when they were delivered to the stores, but it was all a novelty then and I quite enjoyed it. But after about a month it became very repetitive and boring, and I started to dislike the work. Then I was really thrown in at the deep end, because I was put on the parts counter, serving the mechanics with the spares which they needed. It was very confusing because half the time I didn't know what I was looking for, but I soon started to pick it up.

In my first year I did a day-release course at Blackburn Technical College, followed by another year at Tuson Engineering College in Preston. It was a motor-parts course leading to my City and Guilds Certificate; Dutton-Forshaw encouraged me to go on the course and paid my fees. I would like to do the Institute of the Motor Industry's management course (IMI) to learn about the commercial side of the business, but for some reason the company seems to have stopped sending people on that course, which is a shame.

I worked for a brief spell on the trade counter, serving the public and trade customers with parts. When we moved to this building, about eighteen months ago, I was given a job in the phone room, taking orders from small traders and retail customers. When the customer tells me what they want, I make a note of the make and age of the car, and the engine size, so that I can find out the part number. If it is a BL car, I can use our box of microfiche diagrams, which break up every car into its component parts, with their right

Steve collects body wings to supply to the body repair workshop.

numbers. If it is any other make, I have to look it up in the Unipart catalogue.

With all the thousands of different parts which we keep in stock, we're lucky to have a computer to help us keep track of them all. When I've found the part number, I go to the bin-list – a computer print out – and get a computer location which tells me where the part is kept in the store. Once I've found it I book it out, and there is one copy of the order for the customer, and one for our office. The parts are then put in the right bay for delivery by one of our drivers. There are five of us in the phone room, taking orders on five different telephone lines, and most of the time we're all kept fairly busy. Our van drivers cover a large area, and we get orders from all over the West Midlands – I think we must be just about the largest supplier in the North West.

Altogether there are eight of us working with spare parts. I think we're understaffed really, because we get very pushed sometimes, and it's especially hard to keep up with the workload if someone is ill or on holiday. We also have van drivers, clerical staff and reps, but there used to be many more people working in the parts department. If it's very busy I sometimes help out on the counter, but my real job is to take the telephone orders, find the right parts, and get them ready as quickly as possible for collection or delivery.

Talking to a customer at the public counter in the parts department.

Once I've clocked on at 8.30 in the morning, I finish off the previous day's orders, and put the items in the right bays for delivery by the different van drivers. Then I sit at my desk and wait for the phones to start ringing, which usually doesn't take very long! If a customer receives a wrong part, we have to credit him for it, or exchange it for the right one. It's very easy to make a mistake, because in the bins and racks in our stores, we have literally thousands of parts. We must carry at least £400,000 of stock – everything from tiny split-pins to body shells and complete engines of Jaguar cars.

After eating my lunch in the car or the canteen, I might have a game of darts or dominoes or go for a walk around the town.

In the afternoon, we make up the orders for the drivers' second deliveries, and then take orders for the next day. I spend a lot of my working time on the phone, but whether it's on the phone or over the counter, I always get on with people fairly well. That's important in this job, because it can sometimes become very frustrating and you have to know how to keep yourself under control. We are the ones who deal with the public, and they judge Dutton-Forshaw by the way we treat them. We are expected to be courteous, polite and as helpful as possible. That isn't always easy, because some do-it-yourself motorists come in here not really knowing what they want, and keep sending you back to the stores for a nut or a bolt. If you happen to give them the wrong part, they always blame you, even if it was really their fault in the first place.

Although I find the work dull and repetitive sometimes, I enjoy my workmates' company – we have quite a laugh sometimes. Apart from gaining some useful qualifications, my career hasn't really progressed since I started the job, and I don't really see much in the way of future prospects if things stay as they are. I'm considering doing a night-school course in car mechanics, not because I want to be a mechanic, but I think it would help to improve my knowledge of car parts and make me better at my job. It would also make life more interesting if I knew what all the parts were used for, as I'm handling them day after day. It would help me to do my own maintenance on my Mini, too. I get the usual staff discount on parts and petrol, and that's helpful sometimes.

I live with my mum and brother in Preston, and in my spare time I play football and cricket and do a lot of reading – TV doesn't really interest me that much. I get four weeks holiday a year, when I like to go abroad with a few friends – usually to Benidorm, Majorca or Corfu.

I'm paid weekly, in accordance with the National Joint Council of the Motor Vehicle Industry (NJC), but I don't think that the pay is really good enough. I expect more for the work I do, because most of the time we're really busy, and I think we're good at our job. I get a payrise every year until I'm twenty-one, and I'll rise to a Grade 1 pay bracket when I've been here for five years, but I still don't think I have any real future if I stick at this job. Without more qualifications, I can't really hope for promotion to, say, parts mananger. One job I would like to try is that of parts sales rep for Dutton-Forshaw, driving around the area getting business from garages. Reps get a company car and a commission on their sales, and it really does seem like an attractive job to me – perhaps one day I'll get a chance to find out.

Cutting a key for a customer – this service is offered by the parts department.

Steve talks to an account customer on the phone.

Carol Gillybrand

Van Driver

After Carol Gillybrand had passed her driving test she decided to become a van driver. She loves driving and enjoys the freedom that her job at Dutton-Forshaw gives her, calling at different garages, collecting and delivering parts.

I've never been particularly interested in the motor trade, but I enjoy driving and delivery work. Once I'm out on the road, I'm my own boss and I can organize my own working day – it's quite an independent sort of job, really. I used to deliver to chemists' shops, but the people I met on that job were not nearly as friendly as the garage staff who I now deal with on my rounds.

I grew up in Preston, and went to the local secondary modern school, where I took six 'O' levels. I passed three, in English language, English literature, and art, and I wanted to train as a hairdresser when I left school. But I got a job instead, and left it too late to start training – you have to start fairly young to be a hairdresser – and I've changed my mind about that anyway.

When I left school at sixteen, it was much easier to find work than it is nowadays, and I got the first job I applied for, as a shop assistant in a large local department store. It was advertised in the local jobcentre, and I stayed in the job for a year and a half. When I felt like a change, I found another job as a petrol forecourt attendant. After seven months, I was offered the chance of going to London to work as a nanny; I was excited by the idea of moving to London, and jumped at the chance. I enjoyed the work, and had a good time in London, but when the baby started to grow up and I wasn't needed any more, I moved back home and started looking for another job.

Preston seemed very quiet after London, and as I had passed my driving test, I got a job with a pharmaceutical company, delivering to chemists in the North West, as well as working in a pub at nights. Three years later, the company closed down and I found myself without a job. I was unemployed for two months, and then I worked at nights for a newsagent and off-licence shop. One day, in

Carol telephones customers to see if they need anything, before she starts on her round.

the jobcentre, I saw that Dutton-Forshaw needed a van driver for delivering parts, so I sent in an application form. I thought that they would be a good company to work for because they are well known locally, and were likely to be financially secure. My thoughts were right, because I've been here a year now, and I really like the job, the place and especially the people.

I was invited for an interview by the parts manager right away. He told me that he needed a driver for the Liverpool area, and asked me about my previous experience, and my knowledge of local roads. After interviewing a few more applicants, he phoned me the next day to offer me the job. I was really pleased to get another driving job; I think I got it because of my driving experience, and my good knowledge of all the roads in the Liverpool area.

Below *Carol cross-checks the goods with the delivery notes, before setting out on her round.*

Carol receives some final instructions from one of her bosses.

I didn't feel so pleased after the first few days, though. I didn't like the work at all, and thought I'd never be able to do it. Apart from all the paperwork involved, I didn't know one car part from another, and I didn't have a clue where all the garages were on my round. I didn't know any of the people I worked with, either, and getting to know them better was difficult because I was out on the road all day. After about two weeks, though, I began to find my feet in my new job, and I changed my mind about everything once I knew what I was doing.

I had no formal training, but everyone helped to show me the ropes. There are about thirty people working in the parts department, including eight drivers. All the drivers are women, except for one, and we each cover a different area. After a while, my round was changed, and I now cover Southport, Formby and Ormskirk. I prefer my new round because I don't have to drive so far each day before I start my deliveries. I drive a BL Sherpa van, and make about twenty calls a day, delivering everything from nuts and bolts to complete car body panels.

I have to look after the customers in my area, making sure that they get delivery of the right parts on time, and sometimes taking their orders for spares. There are so many different parts for so many different makes and models of car that it is all too easy to make a mistake, so you have to be careful to get it right. My van is my own responsibility, and I have to look after it and keep it clean and in good running order. This involves booking it in for regular servicing, checking the oil, water, battery and tyres, and filling it with petrol each morning.

My usual working day is from 8.45 in the morning until 5.00 p.m., but I'm paid overtime if I get back late because of a breakdown or heavy traffic. After clocking on each morning, I fill the van with petrol from our own pumps, wash it and clean it inside, and go to the office to phone a few customers to see if they need anything. I start checking my orders to see what sort of workload I have for the day, and I write the names of the customers on a board, in the right order for my delivery route. The parts department staff lay out the items in our separate delivery bays, and I check them against my paperwork to make sure that they've got it right. Sometimes the boxes have a wrong part number, or the parts are put in the wrong bays, so careful checking at this stage can save a lot of time later. I load the van in reverse order, so that the last customers' parts are at the front – this makes unloading a lot easier. Sometimes the parts are very heavy, especially bonnets and body panels, so I get someone to give me a hand with them.

If things go well, I leave the garage at about 9.30 a.m., and set off for my first delivery, which is about ten miles away. If a customer has been given the wrong part, I write out a credit-note for him and take the part back to Preston on my return trip. I give each garage a delivery note, and a copy of each is kept in the office at Preston, so that we have a complete record of who has had which parts.

I also collect payment for the parts, whether by cheque or in cash. I'm not allowed to leave the parts without being paid, and I usually collect a few hundred pounds by the end of the day. The morning round always follows roughly the same route, and when I've finished I usually go home for lunch at my parents' house, just outside Preston.

When I get back to Dutton-Forshaw's I sort out the morning's credit notes and other paperwork before loading up for the afternoon round. Sometimes I go to the same customer twice in one day, but the second round usually follows a different route. When I've finished the day's deliveries, I hand in my cash and credit notes to the office, sort out the next day's orders, and park and lock the van before going home.

I still live with my parents, but I'm looking for a house to buy. To help out financially, I work four nights a week in an off-licence, which doesn't leave me with much spare time. But I like to go horseriding at the weekends, I enjoy swimming and playing badminton, and I usually go to a night club in Preston or Manchester on Friday nights. I get four weeks holiday a year, but I can't really afford to go abroad while I'm saving for a house.

Most of my working day is spent out on the road – I must do about six hours driving each day. I spend a lot of time dealing with the customers, who can sometimes be awkward, but usually I enjoy it – most of them are very friendly. The only trouble is that they always seem to want to have a chat on the days when I'm in a real rush! Sometimes they take delivery of the parts, and then ask me to call back later for the money; that can be really annoying and time-wasting. I've broken down once or twice so far, and I hate it. You feels so helpless waiting for someone to come from Preston and rescue you, and it totally messes up the day. Sometimes I have to take back dirty old engines and other faulty parts under warranty, and I'm not too keen on that part of the job either.

Carol loads up her van with parts which have to be delivered.

But I like the driving and the independence of the job – at least I'm out and about, and not stuck in an office. I think that the pay is fairly poor for the work involved, because the job isn't easy. As a van driver, I don't really have any prospects of promotion, but I don't ever see myself working in a shop or office again. I love driving, but I don't have a car of my own, so I'd like to have a job driving a vehicle which I can also use in my spare time. To be fair, the boss occasionally lets me borrow the van for moving furniture etc. at the weekend, and I get staff discounts on any parts which I buy for my family or friends.

Iqbal Patel

Body Repairer

Iqbal Patel left school with CSEs, including metalwork. On an impulse he came into Dutton-Forshaw and filled in an application form for a mechanical apprenticeship. He was offered a job in the workshop, first as a trimmer and later as a body repairer.

I was born in Nairobi, the capital of Kenya, and lived there until I was six years old, when my family moved to England. We came to live in Preston, and I went to the William Temple High School, a secondary modern in Preston. I was already interested in working on cars, and when I left school at the age of sixteen, my five CSEs included a grade 1 in metalwork, which has since proved very useful.

When I started looking for a job, I knew that I wanted to enter the engineering trade, but I wasn't sure about which field I wanted to work in. The school careers office gave me a pile of application forms, and I must have applied for more than forty engineering jobs, mainly apprenticeships with different firms in the West Midlands. But there were too many people chasing too few apprenticeships, and only two companies offered to interview me. Neither of them accepted me, so I started going to college to study for two 'O' levels in English and maths.

I didn't mind going to college, but I still really wanted a job, and kept on sending in applications – I just tried everything I could think of. One day, I was walking past Dutton-Forshaw's garage, and on impulse I just came in and asked the receptionist for an application form for a mechanical apprenticeship. The service manager wrote to me and invited me for an interview, where he gave me some mechanical tests, and asked me a few technical questions about metalwork. I took some examples of my metalwork along to the interview and I think he was quite impressed. After another three interviews, he offered me a job as a trimmer in the service workshop, and I left college and started work right away.

It was all very new to me at first. I was very impressed by the size and facilities of the workshop, but I felt a bit lost until I got used to it all. My workmates used to crack a few

Iqbal refits a headlight to a Jaguar sports car, after the spray shop has finished respraying it.

jokes about my colour, but they were very friendly really, and soon made me feel at home, although I found the work very tiring at first.

To start with, I worked with an experienced trimmer, who showed me the ropes, and gave me the basis of my practical training. After eight months as a trimmer, I did another eight months working on the mechanical side in the workshop. Then I moved to the bodyshop, which is entirely separate from the mechanics' workshops, and started training for my present job as body repairer, or 'tinner' as we call them.

Below *Iqbal smooths down body filler on the back of a Jaguar car.*

The traditional hammer and anvil are still used for panel beating.

Because I had missed out on the first part of the day-release course for apprentices, Dutton-Forshaw sent me to Blackpool Technical College for twenty-four weeks to catch up. The course was a City and Guilds (Part 1), called Craft Studies in Light Vehicle Body Repair, and it was followed by a one-year, day-release course in Body Building, which gave me Parts 2 and 3 of the City and Guilds Certificate. As well as theoretical studies, the courses taught me many practical skills, including welding, and soon afterwards I passed my Skills Assessment test. Dutton-Forshaw paid for all these courses and they still occasionally send me for short training courses which BL give to body repairers when they bring out a new model.

There are three of us 'tinners' in the bodyshop, and we have to carry out repairs to a very high standard, restoring car bodies to their original condition. If the damage isn't too bad, we can beat out any dents, but otherwise we have to remove whole panels and replace them with new ones, usually by welding them in place. When we've got the body in decent shape, it goes to the sprayshop for repainting before it comes back to us to have the lamps, bumpers and any other parts replaced.

When I get here in the morning, I clock on, and have a cup of tea in the 'brew-room' until 8.45 a.m., when it's time to start work. If there's any work left over from the day before, I get on and finish that; otherwise I get a new job-card from the bodyshop manager. We all get on very well – in fact there is a good working relationship in this department. After inspecting the damage on a new job, I have to decide what new parts I need, and then I get them from the store. If a car needs a lot of bodywork, I first have to remove the seats, headlining, bumpers, headlights, and anything else which might get damaged by heat when I'm welding. If I have to fit a new door-shell, I transfer all the trim and fittings from the old one.

I stop for a tea break at about 10.00 each morning, and then work through until lunchtime, when we send the youngest lad out to the chip shop around the corner. After eating our chips, we usually play a few games of cards in the 'brew-room' until it's time to go back to work.

My whole working life is spent in the bodyshop, except when I go to the spares store to

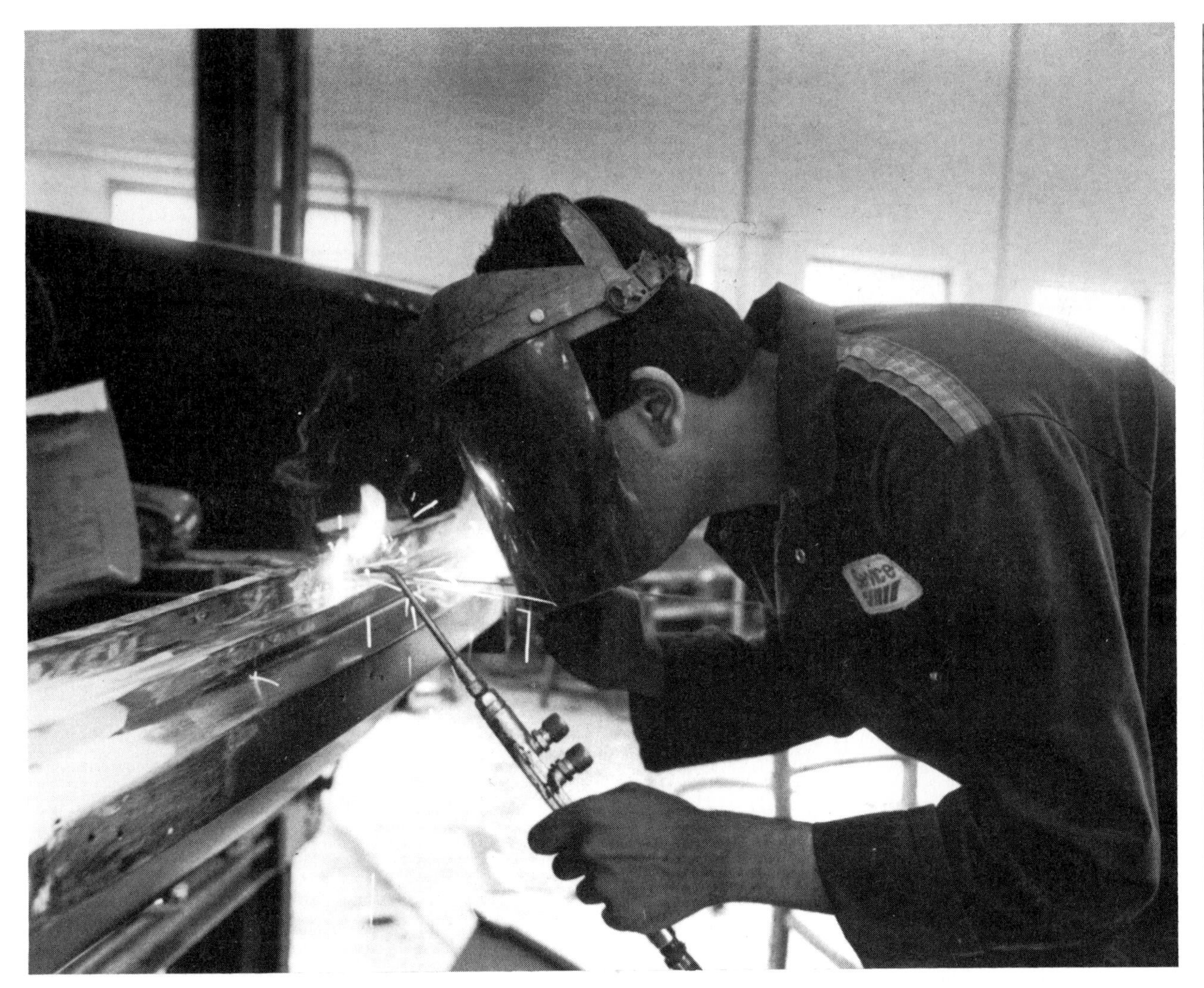

Welding is dangerous work and Iqbal wears a protective mask while he spot-welds a car boot.

pick up a panel or something which I need. The only time I actually get to meet a customer is when someone comes in with a small job which they want done on the spot, but that doesn't happen very often. If the manager isn't around, I sometimes have to work out an estimate of the cost of repairing a damaged car, and I find that quite interesting. I'm happy with the work conditions here, and I've never bothered to join a trade union, because I've never felt the need.

If a dent can be beaten out, I use metal and rubber hammers to restore the panel's original shape. To take the impact of the hammer, we hold blocks of metal – called dollies – behind the panels. A precious tool in this job is a molegrip, which is useful for holding and bending metal and for many other things. We use several compressed-air tools, powered by a compressor, including drills, saws, and chisels, for chopping away the old metal. We still use the anvil and other traditional metal-working tools, but we also have some very sophisticated machinery, such as the body-jig, which straightens out a badly twisted chassis or subframe. Most of these tools are very noisy, and even beating a panel by hand creates quite a din. Sometimes the noise is

Iqbal is lining a Rolls-Royce wheel arch with lead. Lead lining is used on quality cars, instead of the more common plastic fillers.

Assembling a Rolls-Royce door.

almost deafening, so we have to wear earmuffs as a protection.

If a panel is really badly damaged, I have to take it out and weld in a new one. We use three different types of welding equipment, depending on the job in hand. There's oxy-acetylene gas welding, mig welding, and spot welding. Welding is a skilled job, and can be dangerous if you don't know what you're doing – you have to wear heatproof gloves, and a mask to protect your face and eyes.

I find the job really interesting, and I never get bored, because I learn something new every day. I also get loads of satisfaction from my work. To see a badly wrecked car, a real mess, made to look like new as it goes back to its owner, with a gleaming new coat of paint – that really makes me feel good, and to know that we've achieved something worthwhile. I like the workshop and my mates, too. Maybe one day I'd like to try working in another garage, just to see what it's like, but this one seems pretty good to me.

I don't think too much of the basic wage (which is governed by the NJC) considering the amount of work which we put in. On our bonus system we can improve on our basic pay, but I consider that we're highly skilled – not many people could do my job – and skills should be paid for.

Although I enjoy my job, I definitely want to progress from here. I don't want to be a 'tinner' all my life, but at the moment I'm still learning, and I'll just have to wait and see what crops up in the future. Within Dutton-Forshaw, the next step would be promotion to bodyshop manager, but it's a little early to start thinking about that. When a car is damaged in an accident, the insurance company sends round an assessor to examine the damage, and estimate the cost of repairs – I think that must be an interesting job, and I wouldn't mind having a try at it one day.

Andrew Cross
Youth Training Scheme Trainee

Andrew Cross has always wanted to be a mechanic. He tried to get an engineering job after leaving school but had no success. He has just started work at Dutton-Forshaw as a trainee mechanic in the Youth Training Scheme.

Under the Government's new Youth Training Scheme, Dutton-Forshaw acts as a managing agent for the Manpower Services Commission, and this year they took on over one hundred school-leavers in the North West, who they 'farm out' to various garages, both within and outside the Dutton-Forshaw group. I was lucky enough to be one of them, and hopefully my year's broad-based training will stand me in good stead in the future, and give me a better chance of finding a job.

All I've ever wanted to be is a mechanic. I've always enjoyed taking things apart and putting them back together, and for the last twelve months I've been doing up an old Mini in my spare time. I went to a secondary modern school near Preston, where I took eight CSEs including woodwork, technical drawing and engineering science, and passed them all except for English. I applied for seven jobs as a mechanic before I left school this year. The school's careers office told me about six of them, and the other one was advertised in the local paper. I had three interviews, which were really tests of maths and general knowledge, but no-one offered me a job.

I had a part-time job working on a farm near my home, feeding the pigs and cows and driving tractors, but I still wanted to be a mechanic. There were very few vacancies being advertised, and hardly anyone takes on apprentices any more. I was getting bored, and disheartened at the thought of being on the dole with no hope of finding a job, when the careers officer at school told me about the new Youth Training Scheme. I filled in an application form, and about three weeks later I had a letter from Dutton-Forshaw's personnel manager, inviting me for an interview.

They interviewed about 150 lads altogether, and my interview lasted about twenty

Before he started his training at Dutton-Forshaw, Andrew attended an interview with some of the senior managers.

Andrew assists a mechanic, removing a wheel for a puncture test.

minutes. I was asked how I got on with my teachers, and about my hobbies, interests and part-time jobs. I was very nervous and tongue-tied to begin with, but when I started talking about my work on the Mini, I loosened up and was quite happy to talk about something I was interested in. They showed an interest too, both in the Mini and my work on the farm. I managed to show them that I was used to working with my hands, and had some work-experience, and they told me there and then that they'd decided to take me on. I had a formal letter of acceptance, and I started my training here in the Preston garage two weeks ago.

My parents were also invited to the interview, and the personnel manager explained how the Training Scheme worked. He likes parents to understand what's involved and the very real advantages of the Scheme, in the hope that they will support and encourage their sons or daughters during their year's training.

It was nerve-wracking to start with, because I felt lost and didn't know what to do. I didn't know my way around, or any of the people who worked here either. Some of my school-mates were also accepted on the training scheme, but they've been sent to other garages in the area.

I worked on Austin-Morris cars in the workshop, and my first job was to help one of the mechanics to take out an engine. I work with the same mechanic on all sorts of different jobs for four days a week, and I find it's a great way to learn how to do the work. There is a room above the garage which Dutton-Forshaw have converted into a training school, and every Monday I go there for off-the-job training. There is a car up there, and a selection of tools and equipment such as gearboxes, engines, steering assemblies etc. The training officer teaches us special skills,

Trainees examine the working parts of car engines in the training school which they attend one day a week.

but I've only done one day of this training so far. The fifty boys in this area are split into four groups for training, and each group comes here one day a week. Once a week the training officer goes out to the different garages to see how the lads are getting on in their practical, shop-floor training.

I'm not doing any formal course yet, but if I'm lucky enough to be offered a permanent job at the end of this year's training, I hope to go to technical college to take my City and Guilds mechanic's course.

The working day starts with a cup of tea at 8.30 a.m., and then I clock on, put on my overalls, and get a job card from the workshop controller. The mechanic tells me what to do, but my real boss is the workshop manager. I bring the tools to the car which we're working on, and we gradually work through all the points on the job card, with the mechanic explaining what he's doing as he goes along. If we need a spare part, I go to the parts counter, find the parts number and the cost, which I write on the card, take it back to the mechanic and help him to fit it. I'm already trusted to do some things on my own, such as jacking up the cars and removing wheels. This gives me

Removing a timing case so that the mechanic can continue with repairs.

a good feeling inside, because it makes me feel useful, and gives me encouragement for the future, when I'll be looking for a permanent job. The Training Scheme has given me a real chance to find out what work is all about, with perhaps the chance of a career at the end of it.

When we've finished working on a car, we put it away, ready for collection by the owner, hand the job card back to the controller, and get a new one. We stop for lunch at 12.30 p.m. Then I get my lunch from the locker and eat it in the canteen before going for a walk around the town. In the afternoon we work on a few more cars, doing every kind of job you can think of. Because the work is so varied, it's very good experience for me – I'm sure that there's no better way to learn. It's hard work though, and I'm usually pretty tired by the time we finish at 5.00 p.m.

I go home on the bus, which costs me £8.00 per week, but the training officer gives me £4.00 per week towards this. I don't live far enough away to get any more. My wages and travelling expenses are paid by Dutton-

Forshaw, and they are paid back to the company by the Government, in return for my training. It's not much more than I'd get on the dole, but I think I'm far better off doing the Training Scheme – at least I have some hope of a job now, and I'd rather spend my time doing something useful than sitting around at home.

The work also gives me useful experience of handling all a mechanic's tools, such as jacks and air-wrenches for removing wheel nuts, but I'm not yet ready to use some of the bigger machinery in the workshop. In our first week we had an induction course, which really stressed the importance of safety at work. We have to wear overalls, and tough shoes or boots for protection. We've also been told where all the fire extinguishers are, and how to use them if a fire breaks out. Some of the tools and machinery can be very dangerous if you don't know what you're doing, and we're always given very careful instructions before we're allowed to use them.

All I want in life is to be a fully-qualified mechanic in a large garage like this. Everything is still very new to me, but I already feel that I'm beginning to fit in. I don't really know many people yet, but everyone's been very friendly and helpful. I was getting very depressed about not finding a job, but the Youth Training Scheme has given me a sense of purpose, and I'm very grateful for the opportunity to really work with my hands.

To earn some extra money, I still work on the farm at weekends, so I don't really have much time to spare. I work on the Mini on most evenings, and now I'll be able to get a discount on any part which I buy from Dutton-Forshaw, which should be a great help. It would be nice if I was paid more because, although I live with my parents, I get left with very little spare cash out of my wages. I sometimes go to discos with a few friends, but I can't really afford to go out very much, and I'm usually too tired anyway. As a trainee, I'll get four weeks holiday, and I hope that will give me a chance to finish my Mini, and get it on the road.

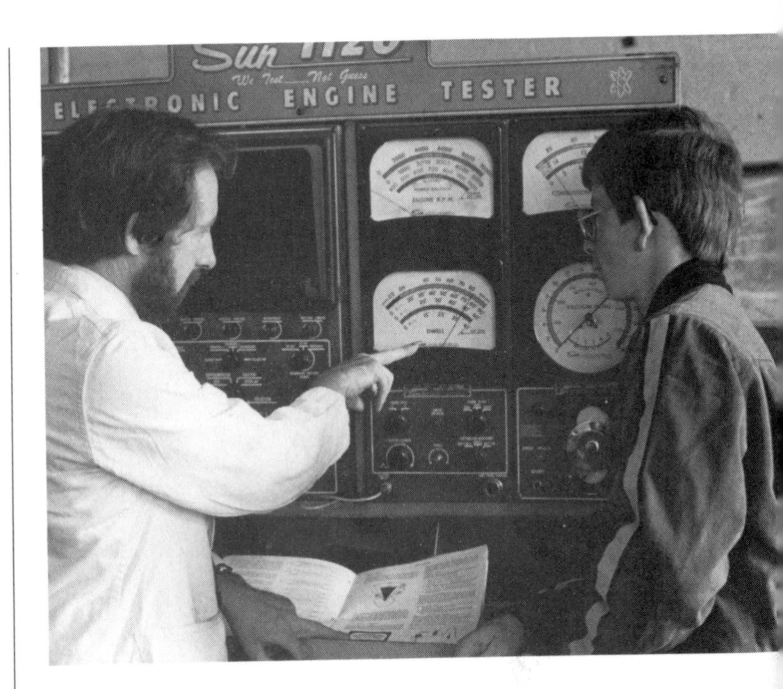

Andrew is told about electronic tuners.

Andrew and the other boys on the Training Scheme study in the training school above the workshop.

Nicola Todd

Trimmer

When Nicola Todd left school she decided to become a mechanic. After an interview with Dutton-Forshaw she was offered a job as a trimmer, repairing the interiors of cars.

Working with cars is seen very much as a man's job, and I'm the first girl ever to work in the service workshop here. When I left school at sixteen, I was a real tomboy, and wanted to be a mechanic, but that was four years ago, and now I'm not so sure. When I get home I'm very tired, filthy and sweaty every day. I feel I'm losing my femininity – I'd like to look, feel and be treated more like a woman. Half the people who come in here think I'm a boy!

I went to a local all-girls school, where I had all the usual girls' vocations pushed down my throat, so the desire to be a mechanic was partly a reaction against this, I suppose. My dad has a plant hire firm, and during the school holidays I used to work in a friend's garage, doing fairly simple jobs on cars. When I was sixteen I decided that I'd had enough of school, but I didn't want to spend the rest of my life sitting in an office. I wanted to keep my dad's business in the family, and asked him to take me on to drive JCBs (earth-movers) and other large machines which he hires out. He didn't like the idea, and said that I'd have to learn a trade first, so that I'd always have something to fall back on.

I had six 'O' levels, including art, and a CSE in maths when I left school, and I had to decide what I wanted to do. The Armed Services are good at teaching trades, so I applied to the Army, Navy and RAF. The RAF were quite interested in me, but I also applied to almost twenty garages. I found their names in the Yellow Pages, and just wrote to them on the off-chance. Most wrote back within a few days, and several of them gave me an interview. Dutton-Forshaw gave me an initial interview and intelligence test, and then invited me back for a second interview with my parents present. They asked me about my mechanical experience, but also included more personal questions about whether I

The trimming/upholstery department where Nicola works.

smoked, and if I planned to get married in the near future. They obviously didn't want to spend their time and money training me, and then see me disappear to get married and raise a family. I'm not sure whether, being a girl, they thought I was capable of doing a mechanic's job, but they must have thought I had something to offer, and that I was seriously interested in cars, because they agreed to take me on as an apprentice trimmer. I was still determined to be a mechanic, but I accepted, and started work almost immediately.

Whereas a mechanic works on the engine, brakes and the like, doing all the heavy work, a trimmer looks after the lighter jobs. I take care of the car's interior – the upholstery, windows, door trimmings, headlining, chrome mouldings, sun roofs, and any niggly little faults, such as water leaking into the car.

At the beginning, I really enjoyed the job because it was different and I felt very enthusiastic about it all. I still wanted to be a mechanic, but I was happy in the workshop. At first the men used to crack a few jokes at my expense, because it was so unusual to see a girl in a car workshop. But they soon got used to me, and before long they were treating me as 'one of the boys'.

She cuts thread before sewing up a car's upholstery.

She removes the headlining from a Mini. First she has to remove all the windows.

When I began my apprenticeship, I worked for three months on the shopfloor to get a basic practical training, then did a six-month course at Blackpool and Fylde College of Further Education. When I came back, I continued the course on a day-release scheme for two years to get my City and Guilds Diploma in Painting and Trimming. In all, I only completed three years of a four-year course, but I still passed.

I started to regret leaving school so early, and began studying history 'A' level at evening class, but the course disbanded through lack of support. I would like more qualifications because young people are coming out of school better qualified than I am, and I really want to move on in life. I've changed my mind about wanting to be a mechanic, but the college course has taught me the skill of re-upholstering car interiors, and I really enjoy doing that. I find it more creative and rewarding than messing about with nuts and bolts and spanners.

The two other trimmers in the workshop are both male, but we all do exactly the same job. There is no sexual discrimination of any kind, and all three of us are responsible for ensuring that our work is properly carried out. My boss is Ian Brown, the service manager. We get on pretty well; he occasionally gives me a right telling off, but only if I deserve it. He treats me in exactly the same way as the men. I don't expect any special treatment just because I'm female, but sometimes it would be nice to have another girl to talk to in this man's world. If I had any problems at work, I'd go and see Mr Brown and get it sorted out. I don't need a trade union to look after me, and I don't really believe in them anyway. I think that they usually cause more trouble than they're worth, and are largely to blame for all the unemployment we have these days. My political ideas are quite

Nicola replaces the door trim on a Rover.

conservative, which most people seem to find a little surprising.

I get a lift to work each morning, and usually arrive at the garage at about 8.45 a.m. After a cup of tea, I queue up with the men outside the workshop controller's office window, to get my first job of the day. He gives me a job-card with a car number and a list of faults to be fixed. I drive the car into the workshop, examine it to see what parts need to be replaced and go to the spares store to fetch them. When the work is finished, I fill out the job-card and write down the time I've taken on the car, and the parts I've used, and give the card back to the controller. He gives me another job-card, which could involve totally different work, and I go through the same procedure. At lunch-time I usually go to the canteen for a game of darts, but if it's a nice day I may go for a walk in the park.

The afternoon follows the same pattern as the morning. Sometimes I get to meet the customers, if they want to show me a certain problem on their car. I like going out and talking to them, but usually, when I'm wearing overalls and covered with grease and glue,

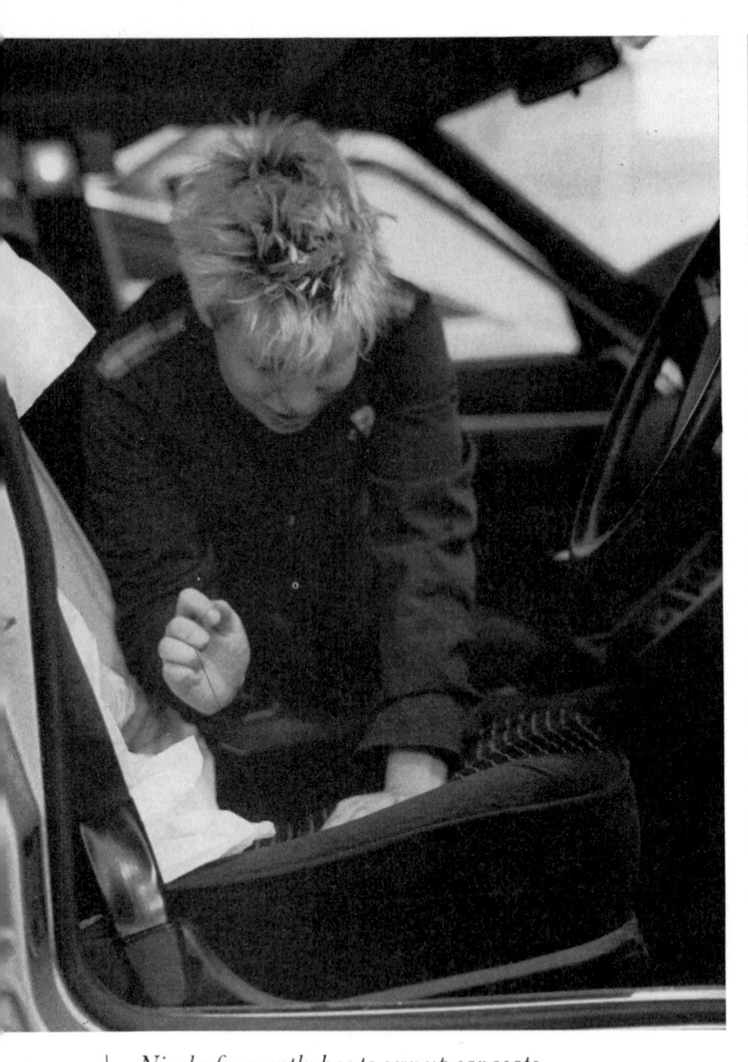

Nicola frequently has to sew up car seats.

In the rest room, Nicola relaxes over a game of dominoes.

they don't even realize that I'm a woman!

I don't use a lot of special tools in my work – hands and patience are the most important tools. I use electric drills fairly often, and if I'm fitting a sunroof into a car I use an electric jigsaw. The workshop foreman comes round at the end of the day to inspect the work; if he gives his approval, the car is ready for the customer to collect.

When I finish work at 5.30 p.m. and go home, I'm always really tired. Trimming may not require as much strength as a mechanic's job, but it's still tiring, physical work. If I've done a lot during the day, and the work has gone well, then I don't mind going home exhausted, because it gives me a sense of achievement. When a car comes into the garage in a real mess, and goes back to the customer looking really smart, that's a good feeling too; it means that even if you don't always enjoy your work, at least you're good at it, and you've managed to please someone!

I feel that I'm quite well paid. I get a fair wage for the work that I do. I could earn even more on the company's productivity-linked bonus scheme, but I'm satisfied with what I get, and I don't think that I could work much faster anyway.

In the future, I don't really see myself going much further in the motor trade. I feel overstretched in my job already, and couldn't handle much more. I've changed a lot in the last four years, and I've become disillusioned with my earlier ideas. My real ambition is to make a lot of money, although I don't yet know how! I'd like to be able to do the best for my young son, as my parents did for me. I'd also love to travel and widen my experience as much as possible. Eventually I might leave the motor trade altogether and try something quite different – perhaps pursuing my interest in upholstery. Now I feel I would like a more feminine occupation.

Gary Bretherton

Foreman, Rolls-Royce Service Section

Gary Bretherton started as an apprentice mechanic at Dutton-Forshaw when he left school. During his apprenticeship he attended courses to gain more qualifications. He now works in the Rolls-Royce section. He loves working on these cars which he says are the best in the world.

I grew up in a little village near Preston. I've always been involved with cars because my dad was a mechanic, and I started tinkering about with them when I was just a boy. I went to the local secondary school, and the five CSEs that I passed were useful in my later training – maths, engineering, commerce, technical drawing and woodwork. I also passed an 'O' level in technical drawing; unfortunately the school didn't do metalwork, which would have been useful as well.

When I was about to leave school, I didn't think at all about going into the motor trade as a career. With my technical drawing qualifications, I could see myself as a draughtsman in a drawing office. But later I thought more about it and the idea of being a mechanic began to appeal to me. Before I left school I approached two firms for jobs – one at Dutton-Forshaw as an apprentice mechanic, and the other as an auto-electrician. The jobs weren't advertised, it was just a shot in the dark really. Both firms gave me interviews and Dutton-Forshaw accepted me as an apprentice while I was still at school.

When I started as an apprentice mechanic, I was working on Austin-Morris cars, but after six months the foreman offered to transfer me to the Rolls-Royce service section, which was then a separate department. I served my five-year apprenticeship, and as well as the practical training and experience which I gained in the workshop, I also attended several courses to get more qualifications. I did a day-release Motor Vehicle Technicician's course (MVT), which was in three parts and lasted five years. I also had to pass the Motor Industry's course. As a result of all my studies, I have a City and Guilds full Technological Certificate, the Service Reception Certificate, and the National Craftsmen's Certificate, as well as associate membership of the Institute of the Motor Industry (IMI).

Gary adjusts the power steering of a Rolls-Royce, using heavy-duty axle stands to keep the wheels off the ground.

Gary discusses worksheets with a colleague in the Rolls-Royce section.

These courses have all been a useful part of my training, and I was encouraged to do them by Dutton-Forshaw, who also paid my fees and expenses.

When I finished my apprenticeship, I started work here as a fully qualified mechanic, repairing and servicing both Austin-Morris and Rolls-Royce cars. After a year, I went to work for another garage who offered me more money. After ten months, Dutton-Forshaw's service manager rang me up and offered me my old job back. I refused at first, but agreed to come back when he offered me the job of chargehand in the Rolls-Royce service section.

A chargehand is a working foreman, and I've been doing the job for four years now. I think I was offered the job because the service manager knew the standards of my work, and because I was the best person around at that time for the job, although I was only twenty-one years old. I had no formal interview, but before I came back I made an agreement with the service manager on the terms of my employment, including pay, conditions of work, and my areas of responsibility. My main reason for coming back was that in the other garage I missed working on Rolls-Royce cars – they are simply the best cars in the world, and a joy to work on. I found my work at the other place boring and repetitive; I had lost all interest in it, which is a bad thing in any job, and I'm glad I agreed to return to Dutton-Forshaw.

In my first few days as foreman, it felt as if I'd never left the place, but I gradually became more involved with running the Rolls-Royce section. I soon realized how different my new job was; it gave me much greater responsibility, and put me in charge of my own worklife.

Although I was very young at the time, I was well qualified for the job because, as well as my ordinary apprenticeship, I had been on several specialist courses at the Rolls-Royce training school, covering all aspects of their range of cars, from the engine to the air-conditioning. Rolls-Royce like us to do a certain number of courses with them every year to keep us up-to-date with the very latest developments on their cars, and they don't like untrained service personnel working on them. I wear a badge on my overalls to show that I'm authorized by Rolls-Royce to carry out any work on their vehicles.

In our small Rolls-Royce service section, which is separate from the rest of the workshop, with its own tools and work-area, I have two other trained mechanics working with me. The work-load varies but in a busy week we sometimes service up to twenty-five cars. As I'm in charge of the section, I have to book in the work when the customers bring in their cars, diagnose any faults, estimate the cost of the parts and labour involved, and ensure the work is completed to a satisfactory standard – Rolls-Royce owners don't like shoddy workmanship! If I have any problems, then I consult my boss, Ian Brown, who is the service manager. We have a good relationship, and I don't feel that I need to belong to a trade union to look after my interests.

When I start work at 8.45 a.m., I first of all sort out the job-cards from the previous day, do any necessary paperwork, and book in the new jobs. Sometimes customers bring in their cars, but often they phone us up, and I have to arrange a time to pick up the car. I share out the day's work between the two other mechanics, and start writing out estimates for each job. Unless it's a routine, straightforward job, estimating can be very tricky; usually we can only give the customer an approximate cost for labour, because we don't know how long each job is going to take.

After a quick coffee break, I take out one or

Fitting an exhaust extraction unit to a Rolls-Royce to prevent poisonous gases filling the workshop.

Gary tightens the exhaust system underneath the Rolls.

Adjusting the carburettor system.

two of the cars for a road test, either to diagnose a fault or to make sure that any work which we've done has been successful. Then I usually go and collect a Rolls from a customer. This can be exciting, because we are occasionally asked to work on a really old, or special model, such as a Corniche or even a Phantom. Most of our customers are local, but I occasionally go to London to pick up a car, and I once had to go to the Isle of Man to do some emergency repairs. But this sort of thing doesn't happen often because Rolls-Royce have a very good worldwide service network, and we usually contact their nearest agent to do the necessary work.

His tool kit is insured for over £2,000.

At 12.30 p.m. the whole shopfloor closes for an hour's lunch break, after which I usually get on with some general mechanical work – such as replacing worn parts, or tuning an engine for maximum efficiency. We carry a large stock of spare parts in our spares department, and I often have to phone them with the code-number of a part that we need. I spend a fair amount of time on the phone every day, dealing with our customers, and with Rolls-Royce Motors, to sort out any warranty problems, or to ask for advice about a particular aspect of a job.

In the rest of the workshop, there are different personnel to look after mechanical, electrical and trim work, but we do all the work on Rolls-Royce cars between the three of us. We all have our own tool kits which we buy from a rep, who regularly visits the garage. Because they are so expensive, it's possible to buy them on hire-purchase and they're well worth looking after. I keep my personal tool-kit in a special metal cabinet, and I've insured it all for £2,000. As well as general mechanical tools, such as spanners, we have a 'rolling road' for diagnosing faults, a Krypton engine analyser to check the timing and electrical performance of an engine, and a large collection of specialist Rolls-Royce tools. Of course, apart from our personal tool-kits, everything else is supplied and paid for by Dutton-Forshaw. I'm responsible for making sure it's all properly maintained and looked after, and I have to ask for replacements if any tools are worn-out or faulty.

Towards the end of the afternoon, I do some more road tests, and look into any difficulties which the other mechanics are having – I enjoy sorting out the problems on any make of car, but even more so when it's a Rolls-Royce.

I am single, and when I finish work at 5.30 p.m., I drive about fifteen miles to the country village where I live with my parents. I drive a Morris Marina, but in my spare time I'm renovating a Triumph TR6 sports car, which I'm really looking forward to taking out on the road. Because I work for Dutton-Forshaw, I get a staff discount on any spare parts I need, which is a real help in keeping down the cost of the project.

I sometimes play snooker, but cars are my whole life really. When I'm not working on my own car, I often help friends with theirs, and I do a fair amount of rally-driving. My main interest is 'classic' cars – the sporting cars of the 1950s, '60s, and '70s. The only time I put cars out of my mind is when I go abroad on holiday.

I really enjoy my job, not the paperwork so much, but the mechanical, practical side of working on these beautiful cars. I couldn't do the job if I didn't enjoy it. Unlike a production line in a factory, you have to be interested in this work to do it well, and I've always tried to learn as much as possible, and to keep up with modern developments on every make of car.

I don't consider myself well-paid, and I don't really get any extra perks in the job. The company has many overheads to pay for, of course, but I still feel that I deserve a little more for the work that I put in.

Within Dutton-Forshaw, the next logical step in my career would be promotion to service manager, but I don't think that I'd enjoy it; there's too much paperwork and administration involved, and I'm more interested in the practical, mechanical side of the work. Eventually, I'd like to have my own repair business, specializing in Rolls-Royce and other 'exclusive' cars, such as Jaguars, Porches, Bentleys and Mercedes. I would also love to be able to afford my own Rolls-Royce. They are, without a doubt, the best cars in the world. No matter what other car companies may claim, for design, workmanship and sheer style, there is only one Rolls-Royce!

Gary test drives 'the best car in the world'.

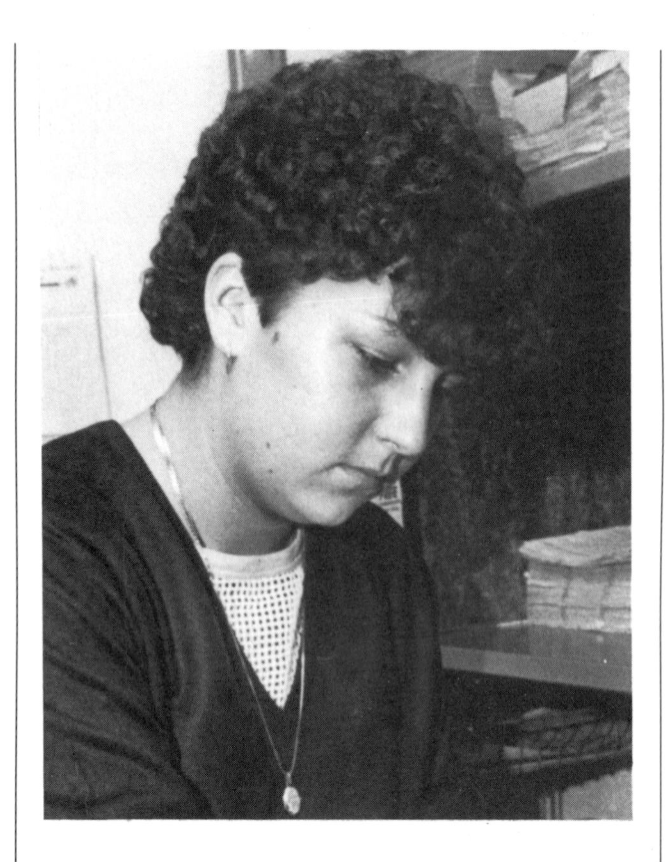

Jackie Davis

Parts/Costing Clerk

After a six-month period at Dutton-Forshaw on a Youth Opportunities Programme, Jackie Davis was asked to stay on as a full member of staff. Her work involves contact with the customers and also dealing with cash.

I first decided that I wanted to be a secretary when I was about thirteen. I don't really know why I wanted to do secretarial work, but it certainly wasn't parental influence, because my dad sells pigs, and my mum works in a shop. At that time I wasn't at all interested in the motor trade, and I imagined myself working in a bank, or a travel agent's office, or something similar.

I went to a mixed comprehensive school just outside Preston, and left when I was sixteen, with eight CSEs and two 'O' levels, in maths and housekeeping. After school, I went to Tuson College in Preston, for a year, doing a full-time Business Studies course, which led to a diploma. As part of the course I took two exams in typing – UCLI Grade 1, and the Pitman exam, for which you have to be able to type forty-five words a minute. The course also included a two-week 'work-experience' placement with a local company, and I came here, to Dutton-Forshaw. They asked me to come back at the end of my course to work for six months on a Youth Opportunities Programme. I still wasn't sure what I wanted to do when it came to looking for a permanent job, but the problem was solved for me, because at the end of my six months here, I was asked to stay on as a full member of the staff.

During my original two weeks' placement at Dutton-Forshaw, they must have thought that I had potential, otherwise the parts manager wouldn't have asked me back for six months. Mum and Dad thought it was a good idea, as a way of getting more work experience, which would make me more attractive to future employers. After the six months, there were redundancies in some departments of the company and I wasn't at all sure that I'd be asked to stay on, but they decided that they wanted to keep me. I was very pleased, because although I had been looking for other

The parts and cost accounting room where Jackie works.

jobs, I really wanted to stay here. I liked the work and got on with everybody fairly well, and didn't like the idea of having to leave at all.

I felt very differently when I first came here, though. The first few days were awful, because I didn't know anyone and wasn't too sure what I was meant to be doing. Learning the job in college and doing it for real are very different. In the office, you can't afford to make mistakes, and sometimes you are under real pressure to get through the work quickly and efficiently.

I thought I'd learnt everything at college, but I've learnt an awful lot more here. Now I'm more confident, and can mix with people easily, and I can see how the whole company works, and what the business world is all about. During my six months on the Youth Opportunities Programme, I was also trained to use the switchboard, handling incoming and outgoing telephone calls. It seemed very complicated at first, and I never thought I'd be able to manage it, but now I find it easy and actually enjoy it. It makes a change from typing now and again, and it's always useful to have another office skill.

I work with four others in the parts office, and we all get on very well. We have one girl on the new Youth Training Scheme, who does mainly typing and filing while she is learning the job. Another girl batches all the documents to be fed into the computer in our office, or to be sent to a data-bank in Birmingham. A third girl looks after customers' credits for spare parts, operates the computer, controls the stock of parts in the shop, and does the staff wages. We also have a man who is in charge of all the office accounts and chasing up bad debts.

Most of my time is taken up with handling

She looks up old invoices of parts used for car repairs.

the takings from our sales of spare parts. Every night I empty the till in the shop, put all the money and cheques into a bag, and give it to the parts manager to put in the night safe bag. When I tip out the bag on to my desk the next morning, it is all a big jumble of notes, coins and cheques. After dividing the cash into different piles of notes and coins, I start counting. I do the coins first, to get them out of the way, and enter the total on a sheet which is divided into columns for different notes and coins. I then do the same with the notes, starting with the biggest, and working my way down to £1 notes. After carefully looking at the cheques to see that they're correctly signed and dated, I count up their total value, using a calculator, and enter them on the sheet as well. When I've worked out the grand total of the previous day's takings, I have to check this against the cash-sales receipts for the day. If the two don't balance, then I have to check through everything for a possible error. I usually find that, by checking the till-roll, someone has made a mistake in ringing up the VAT surcharge. The amount of money involved is usually around £1,000, and it sometimes takes me most of the day to add it up and balance it against the receipts, using my desk-top calculator.

When this is finished, I have to bag up the takings to go to the bank. Some of our customers – the larger local garages – have a monthly

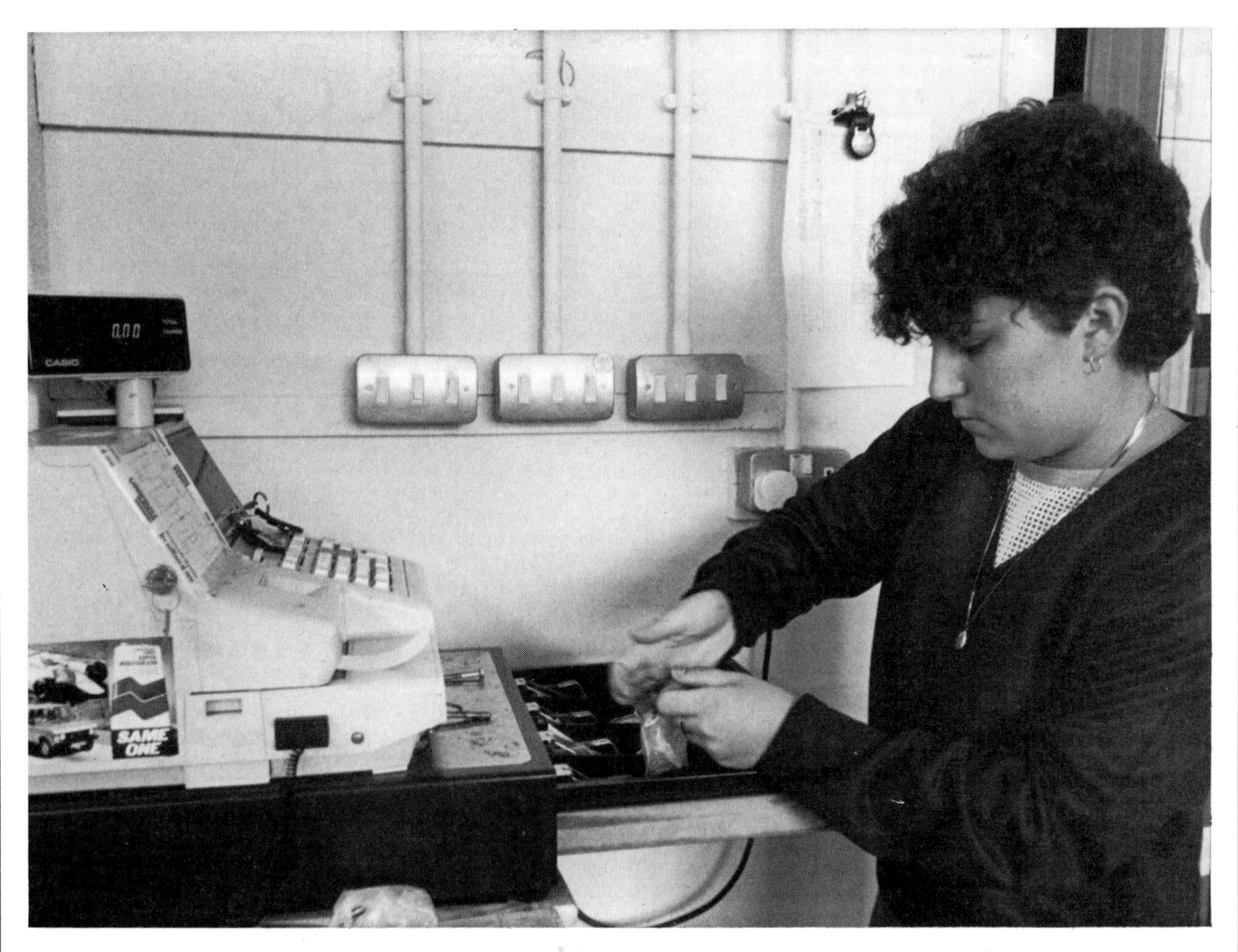

account with us, and I have to balance their cheques and send them for banking as well.

We share the typing between us, and whoever has time types letters to customers, asking for overdue payments, internal memos about general staff policies, and letters to job applicants. We also deal with any administration in the parts department, and we have to file all the cash-sale receipts and the computer records of parts sales.

The office staff don't have to clock on each morning, but I usually arrive at 8.30 a.m. Whoever arrives first puts on the kettle, and we have a cup of tea before starting work at 8.45 a.m. By that time, the manager has already put the cash bag on my desk, and I start counting the money. We have a mid-

Jackie empties the till in the parts shop.

Jackie takes cash out of the safe to provide floats for the tills in all the departments of the garage.

She occasionally works on the telephone switchboard in the showroom.

morning tea break, and for lunch I usually eat in the office, and read a magazine. In the afternoon, I carry on checking the receipts, and it takes most of the rest of the day to balance the receipts against the takings. The delivery van drivers come back just before 5.00 p.m. with all their money and receipts, which are put in the till. After emptying the till and making sure that the money is put in the night safe bag, my day's work is finished, and I catch the bus home.

I really have two jobs here, because on Saturday mornings I work for four hours in the parts shop, behind the counter and on the switchboard. I take the money and give change – it gives me a chance to meet the customers, which I enjoy. It makes a change for me, and it's well paid – I'm paid an overtime rate of time-and-a-half, which means that I get six hours' pay for four hours' work. I'm the only one in the office who isn't married, and I don't mind giving up one morning of my weekend. It's something different for me, and it provides some useful extra cash to spend on clothes, holidays, and going out in the evenings. At the end of the morning, the takings are put in the night safe bag with Friday's money, ready for me to count on Monday morning.

Jackie counts up the cash.

I like the people at Dutton-Forshaw and I find the work interesting. I never do the same thing all day, and there is always some little problem which I have to solve. I don't consider myself well-paid, and I don't earn as much as some of my friends who do similar jobs elsewhere. But I'm still better off than some, and I have no real complaints. I work in a local village pub two nights a week, and this, together with my overtime, brings my earnings up considerably. On the whole, I manage quite well. I live with my mum in a village not far from here, and apart from working in the pub, I like going to discos occasionally. I get four weeks holiday a year; I've just come back from Spain, and I want to go abroad again soon.

Although I enjoy my job, I want to move on in life, and my main ambition is to be a private secretary. It's a job which often needs shorthand, so I want to go to night-school to learn this extra office skill. Dutton-Forshaw are a good firm to work for, and I hate the thought of leaving the people I work with, but I think that eventually I may have to move on if I want to find a better job.

Ian Brown

Service Manager

Ian Brown came to Dutton-Forshaw as an apprentice twenty-five years ago. After his apprenticeship he became a mechanic and later a service reception engineer. His wide experience has led to his promotion, four years ago, to service manager at the Preston branch.

I have spent my whole working life with Dutton-Forshaw, although they were trading under a different name when I started my apprenticeship, twenty-five years ago. I went to a small local country school, and when I left at the age of fifteen, I knew that I wanted to work with cars, and to be trained as a mechanic: that was my one ambition as a lad. My father was a local businessman, and he encouraged my interest in the mechanical side of the motor trade. When he came to this garage to buy a new vehicle, he made enquiries about apprenticeships, and I was taken on shortly afterwards.

I had no qualifications when I left school, but they weren't really necessary in those days for an apprentice mechanic. To ensure a steady supply of trained mechanics, the company used to take on several lads every year to serve their traditional five-year apprenticeship. At first I only earned £2.50 a week, but I was thoroughly trained in every aspect of a mechanic's job. Now apprentices are fairly well paid, but they have really priced themselves out of work – companies can no longer afford to train and employ them, and these days we don't take on any apprentices here at Dutton-Forshaw.

During my apprenticeship, I did a night-school course in car mechanics, and when I was fully trained I worked here for four years as a mechanic. Then I left the workshop floor and became a service reception engineer. I still worked on the cars, but the new job gave me more responsibility; I had to deal with the customers when they brought their cars in for service or repairs, sort out what work needed to be done on each vehicle, and write out the job sheets for the mechanics to do the work.

The next step in my career was promotion to workshop controller, handing out the work to the various mechanics and 'progressing'

Ian's office, situated above the workshops, gives him a clear view of everything that is happening.

the work – following it through all its stages to completion.

These different jobs gave me a good working knowledge of every aspect of the garage's service department, and it seemed the logical next step when I was promoted to service manager, four-and-a-half years ago.

When the previous service manager left, I didn't automatically get his job. The post was advertised in the press, and I made a written formal application. I felt that I was as capable of doing the job as anyone else, having worked my way up through the ranks of the service department. I was a little apprehensive when I went to the interview, but the questions I was asked were all relevant to the job, and I had no trouble in answering them. Dutton-Forshaw must have felt that my previous experience with them would enable me to fulfil the demands of the post, because I was offered the job a few days later.

At first I was excited by the challenge of increased responsibility, but I also felt a certain amount of pressure from having to deal with the new situation. I was still working in the same place, with the same people, but in a different role. To help me meet these new challenges, the company enrolled me on a series of management and supervisory training courses. Both BL and Rolls-Royce run such courses, and I was awarded a diploma when I completed them. Dutton-Forshaw encourages us to attend these courses, and they pay all our expenses, because it is in their interest to promote our managerial skills – better managers mean higher profits!

As service manager, I'm responsible for a fairly large slice of the garage's operations. We have a large workshop, employing twenty staff, who handle about forty cars a day. As well as the mechanics, the workshop staff includes trimmers, who look after minor bodywork and upholstery problems, and testers who make sure that the quality of workmanship is up to scratch. The workshop foreman advises on work in progress, and the workshop controller gives the work to the mechanics and follows it through to completion. A small team of specially trained mechanics work exclusively on Rolls-Royce cars. They have their own tools and their own area of the workshop. Customers are dealt with by the service receptionists, and the cost-office staff work out a price for each job, do all the accounting, and send out the bills. We also have a warranty office, which processes bills to manufacturers for work done on cars which are still under their guarantee.

I live on the outskirts of Preston, so I drive in to work each morning in the company car (a BL car of course!) which is one of the 'perks' of my job. I usually get here by about 8.10 a.m. when I check around the workshop to make sure that everything is OK to start the day's work. Between 8.30 and 10.00 a.m. is a busy time, as customers drop in their cars on their way to work, so I usually help out in reception for an hour or so. I enjoy meeting the customers, and we always try to do everything we can to help them. As a service department, we have to live up to our good

Any major service and repair problems which a customer may have are dealt with by Ian.

reputation, and a satisfied customer means future work for all of us.

When the early morning rush has eased, I go to my office to open the mail and deal with any outstanding paperwork. After handling a few customer enquiries on the telephone, I check with the workshop controller that all the work in hand is progressing smoothly, before having a quick coffee break. After this I sometimes telephone the car factories to obtain authority from BL or Rolls-Royce to carry out certain work on one of their models. I look after any problems which customers may have in obtaining spare parts from manufacturers, and sometimes arrange for factory personnel to come to the garage to inspect any problem vehicles for which we need assistance.

If I have time, I go home for lunch, but sometimes I have to grab a sandwich, or miss lunch altogether on a really busy day. In the afternoon I check on the progress of the various jobs – when you're working on forty or so cars a day, tight progress control is essential. When the day's problems have been sorted

Ian tours the workshop.

out, I finish writing my letters, and get the mail ready for posting. I share a secretary with the garage's general manager, but I do most of my own paperwork. We officially finish work at 5.30 p.m., but I usually end up working for an hour or so after everyone has gone home. When I do get home, I might do some gardening, or tie some fishing flies. Television doesn't interest me – I'd much rather be out in the open air. I enjoy fishing, cycling with my wife in the local countryside, or walking in the Lake District, which isn't too far away from here.

One of my responsibilities as manager is the hiring of new staff, whenever we have a vacancy within the service department. If I need a new mechanic, for instance, I place an advertisement in the local paper, and interview the best applicants. What I look for in a mechanic is a first-class operator with a proven track record; but as well as experience, I also look for someone with the best qualifications I can find to fill the available post.

As well as hiring people, I also have to fire them occasionally. If anyone has been with us for less than twelve months, and I'm not happy with their standard of workmanship or attitude to the job, it is no problem because, by law, I can dismiss them. But if someone has been with us for a long time, I first go through all the normal warning procedures before consulting our general manager. It isn't a pleasant task to dismiss anyone, and thankfully, I have only had to do it twice in my five years in this job.

Paperwork is a more persistent problem, because it always generates more paperwork, and seems to take up a lot of my time. For example, if I am answering a letter from a customer whose car we have repaired or serviced, I have to research my answer thoroughly, and find the relevant job card, which gives details of work, the cost, the date and who carried it out. Paperwork has a habit of mounting up if you don't keep on top of it, but it's a part of the job, and something that has to be done.

Generally, though, I like my work because it presents a challenge. I enjoy sorting out the jobs which are not running smoothly, and I like the contact that I have with other people. The company is a good one to work for, and all the staff receive certain benefits, including discounts on cars, petrol, spare parts and servicing. There is also a sports and social club which is generously supported by the company, but, to be honest, I don't make much use of it. My managerial position demands more commitment than was expected of me when I worked on the shopfloor, but it also provides more in the way of 'perks'. Apart from the increased salary and the company car, which is very useful, I receive full pay when I am sick, and the company also pays my subscription to BUPA, a private healthcare scheme.

As for the future, I would be quite happy to carry on doing a good job in my present position. I'm not expecting to progress much further in the motor trade – as service manager in a large garage, I am already at the top of my particular tree. I suppose I could always go into another line of business as a manager, either within or outside the motor-trade, but I don't really have any ambitions in that direction.

He discusses a problem on a new car with the sales manager.

Ian discusses the spare parts stock with the manager of the department.

Alan Barnard
Service Receptionist

When Alan Barnard left the RAF after many years as a maintenance engineer, he wanted to work in the civilian side of the motor trade. His job as service receptionist at Dutton-Forshaw brings him into contact with customers, which he finds very rewarding.

My whole working life has been spent in the world of transport and motor maintenance. This is my second career, really, because I worked for twenty-five years in the RAF before getting a civilian job in the motor trade.

I'm a West Country man, and I grew up in Bristol – I still like going back there for holidays when I get the chance. I went to an elementary school in Bristol, but I didn't take any exams. I had to leave and find a job when I was fourteen, to earn money to contribute to the family income. Like most of my school pals, I was interested in engineering, and after working for a friend for a while, I got a job with what was then the Ministry of Supply, maintaining military vehicles.

I joined the RAF in 1942 and worked for three years as an aero-engineer, servicing transport and fighter planes, before returning to road transport maintenance. While I was in the RAF I had a thorough training in motor maintenance, and took several promotional exams, including a complete course in Trade and Administration for transport maintenance. I travelled widely and worked as an RAF maintenance engineer at home and abroad, until 1974. I was near the end of my service time anyway, so I applied for voluntary redundancy.

I already knew Preston pretty well and I liked the town, so I decided to come here to live. Dutton-Forshaw were advertising in the local press for a service receptionist, and I decided to apply, because it sounded like an interesting position which would give me an insight into the workings of the civilian side of the motor trade. A few days after my application, they invited me for an interview, which went very well. I was asked about my background and experience, my attitudes to work and life in general, and I must have given the right answers, because I was offered

The service reception area where Alan works.

the job a few days later, and started work almost immediately. I was quite used to interviews after being in the RAF so it didn't cause me any problems of nervousness and the like. My maturity, ability to get on with people, and a strong sense of responsibility were all factors which I think helped to win me the job. The discipline and experience which I gained in the RAF also probably played a part in Dutton-Forshaw's decision to employ me.

The RAF and the civilian motor trade are two totally different worlds, and I found the first few days a little strange, but from the very beginning I enjoyed the job. To help me to do the job properly, the company sent me on manufacturers' training courses for service receptionists, run by BL and Rolls-Royce. These lasted between three days and a week, and I still go to familiarization courses when either firm brings out new models which we will have to deal with. I've been doing the same job for nine years now, and I'm quite happy with it – I'm not really interested in promotion or any other changes in my working life. However, the job itself has changed since I first started, particularly with regional to the financial side of customer relations. Because of increasing costs of labour and parts, the customer is now much more selective about which garage to use, and what work he wants done – which means that we have to be much more competitive than we used to be.

Checking the oil in a customer's car.

Alan discusses the problems of a customer's car and assesses the repairs necessary, with the chief road tester.

The reception staff have a hand in the whole service process, from beginning to end. We are the public face of the service department; the customers hardly ever see the mechanics themselves, and all the custom is managed through us. If anything does go wrong, we're always the people who bear the brunt of it from the customer, either in person or over the telephone.

You can't really watch the clock in this job, and I work from 8.10 in the morning until the last customer goes home at night, although I'm usually finished by 6.30 p.m. Most of my working day is spent in contact with the customers, who either phone us up or call at reception in person if they need service or repair work done on their car. I have to arrange for the work to be done at a time when the workshop can handle it, and when it is convenient to the customer. In reception we effectively control the workshop hours and workload, because we have to estimate the man-hours needed for each job. On the agreed day, I make out a job card for the work, and fill out the other necessary documents, depending on whether the car is still under warranty or the customer is paying for the work himself. All the paperwork is then given to the workshop controller, who manages the manpower on the shopfloor, and he assigns the job to a mechanic.

During the progress of a job, unforeseen problems on a car often come to light. These are reported back to us in reception, and we then have to contact the customer for his instructions – whether he wants us to replace a badly-worn gearbox, or fit new exhaust mountings, for example. The instructions are then passed back to the shopfloor, and when the work is completed it is tested and passed by the controller. The paperwork then goes to the costing department (either the retail or the warranty side) to work out a price for the job. It all then comes back to us, with a completed bill, and when the customer turns up to collect his vehicle, it is purely a matter between him and reception. We do occasionally have to deal with awkward customers, but that is something which you have to take in your stride. It is all a matter of self-control and personality really, which is something no textbook or training course can teach you.

We're also involved in the progressing of parts receipts, if a customer wants a spare part which we don't have in stock. We order the part from the manufacturer, tell the customer when it has arrived and arrange a time for it to be fitted. The cost-office staff usually make out the bill, but if they're too busy or not available, we do it ourselves, taking both parts and labour into account.

If a customer needs some bodywork done on his car, we refer him to the bodyshop, to deal direct with the manager there. But apart from the bodyshop, my job as a receptionist involves me in almost every aspect of the garage's activities, as we handle every kind of mechanical or electrical fault on a vehicle. I enjoy this variety, and the insight which it gives me into the whole business. The personal contact with the customer I find very rewarding, because I enjoy meeting people and trying to help them. I wouldn't do the job if I didn't enjoy it, and my only real ambition now is to stay fit enough to work until I retire. The only thing I don't like is handling the occasional tricky customer who is quite happy for anyone to pay the bill for his work except himself. Customers can also get very irate if their car isn't ready on time.

I have four weeks' holiday a year, and I consider that I'm fairly paid for the work that I do. I own a car, and Dutton-Forshaw allow me staff discounts on various services, but that is the only real 'perk' of the job. I live in a bungalow in the suburbs of Preston, and when I'm not working, I like to get out into the surrounding countryside as much as possible. All in all, I'm quite happy with my lot, and my long career in the motor industry has been both interesting and enjoyable.

Arranging with the workshop controller for a customer's car to be repaired.

Helping out at the workshop spare parts counter.

Hugh Duckworth

Sales Manager

Hugh Duckworth finds his job as sales manager of a busy motor company branch office challenging and rewarding. He enjoys the contact he has with staff and customers, and with the marketing side of the motor industry as a whole.

I've always been interested in cars, and started messing about with them when I was a young lad. My parents sent me to a grammar school near Oldham. There I passed seven 'O' levels, but I didn't work hard enough at my 'A' levels, and I only passed economics before I left school at the age of eighteen. My father was a salesman too, on the technical engineering side of a company which made machinery for the textile industry. He encouraged me to go to the Bolton Institute of Technology, where I did a two-year HND course in business studies.

At the end of the course, I still had a strong interest in cars, and wanted to go into the car manufacturing industry. I applied for about twenty jobs on the marketing side of the industry, as a trainee salesman. Not all the jobs were in the car industry, and some of them weren't even advertised – I just sent in applications in the hope that there might be some vacancies. About eight companies showed an interest in me, and gave me interviews. ICI offered me a job as a market research assistant in their plastics division. I left college when I was twenty, and during the eighteen months that I worked for ICI, I took the Diploma of the Institute of Marketing.

I wasn't really interested in plastics, though, and because I didn't feel involved with my work, it became very boring. I still wanted to work with cars, so I made a speculative application to Dutton-Forshaw. They were obviously puzzled at first as to why I wanted to make such a complete change, from selling plastics to selling cars, and at the interview they were really testing my commitment and interest. But they agreed that, if I was prepared for a challenge, they would take me on as a management trainee – the managing director who interviewed me must have decided that I had potential and was worth a risk.

I started in 1972, and the first few days were very different – I felt a mixture of nervousness and excitement. I spent the first six months as personal assistant to the general manager here in Preston. It was a very good experience because it gave me an insight into the whole business, and I was really glad to be working with cars at last.

The next part of my training was to work for three months in each department of the garage – sales, service, and parts. I also went on about half a dozen formal training courses, run by BL or Rolls-Royce. These courses, which were paid for by Dutton-Forshaw, generally lasted about a week, and I passed the exams at the end of each one.

I then worked as an assistant for the Rolls-Royce sales manager, handling most of the administration. I found it really interesting because we were closely involved with the Rolls-Royce factory. It also prepared me for the next step – a fully-fledged car salesman at last! I was transferred to another, smaller branch, near Preston, as their Jaguar salesman. This worked out very well indeed, and I was really bitten by the sales bug at this point. To do the job well, you need plenty of confidence, as well as knowing the vehicle models inside and out. But I think the secret of success in the world of car sales is understanding

Hugh holds a weekly sales meeting in his office.

He helps a salesman to value a second-hand car for sale.

and 'reading' the people you're dealing with.

Having proved to Dutton-Forshaw that I could sell cars, I moved back to Preston as specialist sales manager for Rolls-Royce and Jaguar. At that time, another company with the group required assistance with its sales in London, so I worked there for six months. When I came back, I was made assistant sales manager for all car sales, and eighteen months ago, after an informal interview with the managing director, I took over as sales manager here.

It's a demanding job, with a lot of responsibility, but I find it very rewarding. As manager, I'm now in charge of two junior managers, ten salesmen, five clerical staff, and the drivers and cleaners. As well as the new cars in the showroom, we buy and sell used cars of any make if they're in good condition. I have to value the vehicles we take in part-exchange deals, and if they're too old or in too poor a condition for us to sell to the public, I have to arrange for their disposal, usually to traders or car auctions. At Dutton-Forshaw, we act as distributors for BL and Rolls-Royce cars, supplying seven other dealers in this area.

Both our company and the manufacturer set sales forecasts which I have to meet. These days, with such fierce competition and such low profit margins, a high turnover is essential, which is why fleet sales are so important to us. We contact local companies, such as bakeries and factories, who may be using anything from three to four hundred vehicles and offer them lower prices in return for bulk orders. We have a special salesman to quote prices for the larger national contracts with police forces, local authorities and the like, and it is this high volume/low profit business which helps us to maintain such a high turnover. In any one year, we usually sell about 2,000 new cars and about half that number of used vehicles.

As you can imagine, it's a fairly complicated business handling that number of vehicles. We order them on a monthly basis, and we have a computer to help us with our stock control. Our computer terminal is linked to BL's central computer, which covers

Hugh takes stock of the new cars in the compound at the rear of the garage.

Hugh assesses the value of a part-exchange car which has come into the garage.

the entire distribution network over the whole country. Using this, we can locate the precise car which a customer wants, even down to the colour, in less than thirty seconds! I also have a secretary and a sales administration manager to help me with stock control and the mountains of paperwork involved in selling cars.

An important part of my job is to encourage and motivate my staff. We set monthly sales targets for the salesmen, and carefully monitor their performance. Their wages are linked to their unit sales, whereas mine are linked to the profitability of my whole sales department. If a salesman fails to meet his target for three consecutive months, we review his position in the company, but they are all well trained, and should be able to meet their targets.

When taking on new staff, I prefer young people with no experience. The older generation of salesmen are often outdated in their approach, and to achieve the high volume sales which we need, we have to have a new breed of young salesmen. When we interview applicants, we are looking for people who can sell themselves; if they can do that, we can train them to sell cars. They need an outgoing

Hugh's office overlooks the showroom where one of the salesmen is advising a young couple about the purchase of a new car.

personality, and plenty of confidence if they hope to be able to cope with the modern, aggressively competitive world of car sales.

My office looks on to the showroom, so it's easy for me to keep in touch with the public and the salesmen. I have to control their deals and decide on profit margins. Most of the year we have a steady trade, but there are two annual sales peaks, which cause enormous problems. One peak is in January, because a vehicle's year of registration affects its second-hand value when the owner decides to sell. But the biggest peak is in August, with the annual change in number registration. Everyone wants a car with the new number plate, and so they wait until August to buy. In that one month we usually do two or three month's business – it's our busiest time by far.

I spend a fair amount of my working life out of the office, visiting Rolls-Royce customers, fleet customers, manufacturers, and attending sales conferences. I also go on training courses for new models, and I devote a lot of time to marketing. We have special sales promotions in the showroom which are linked to national advertising campaigns, and we often invite customers along to the showroom for social evenings during these promotions. We sponsor point-to-point horse races, and we like to invite customers to those as well. Mine is certainly not a nine-to-five job, and it demands total commitment from me, but I don't mind that.

I am fairly well paid, but my salary really depends on my performance – the more I sell, the more I get. I also have a company car, free health and life insurance, and a good holiday entitlement. We have a sports and social club, and I usually organize our Christmas functions and the annual dinner-dance. I don't have a lot of spare time, but I have quite an active social life, and enjoy swimming and going to weekend horse events. I always look forward to going abroad on my annual holiday – usually to Greece or Portugal.

As a salesman, I sometimes get frustrated at the occasional lack of support from the car manufacturers. When they don't make enough cars, it causes supply problems for us, and sometimes I feel that they are not making enough of the right models for the markets available. Apart from that, I like my job. If I had stayed in industry, I would never have had the level of responsibility which I now have. I enjoy the contact which I have both with staff and customers, and I like being at the sharp end of the selling process. The sales department makes a very visible, easily perceived contribution to the business as a whole – every car sold is a success.

In the future, I can see my career progressing through the group structure of Dutton-Forshaw, and the next obvious step would be promotion to general manager. I could get an equivalent post in the group's national organization, or possibly join another company, or even work for the manufacturers. But whatever happens, I want to stay on the marketing and sales side of the business, rather than get involved in pure administration.

David Lyon
Managing Director

David Lyon was asked to join the company when he was working on the audits in his capacity as chartered accountant. He defines his responsibilities, in his present job of regional managing director, as producing a profit, satisfying his customers and motivating his 350-strong work-team, all of which he finds challenging and enjoyable.

My involvement in the motor trade developed fairly late in my career, after I had already worked for fourteen years with a local firm of chartered accountants. I went to Kirkham Grammar School, seven miles from Preston, and as a schoolboy, I wasn't particularly interested in the car business. My family lived in a rural village, and I passed eight 'O' levels, including agricultural science. I stayed on at school and joined the sixth form to take 'A' levels in maths, history and French. My best subject though, and the one which I most enjoyed, was maths, and after the first year of the sixth form, I decided to leave school to become articled to an accountant.

My father was the local schoolmaster and through his contacts in this area I had interviews with three local firms. All offered to take me on, but I accepted a job with a long-established Preston firm, who offered me a wage (of 75p per week!) during my five years as an articled clerk. The others wanted me to pay them a premium for my training, which was the common practice in those days.

While I was an articled clerk, I studied to obtain my qualifications through correspondence courses four night a week. After qualifying as a chartered accountant in 1958, I worked for a year with the same firm. This was just before the end of National Service, and I was called up to join the armed forces in 1959. For two years I was a training officer, serving as second lieutenant in the Royal Army Pay Corps. When I left the Army, I came back to Preston and rejoined the same firm of chartered accountants.

After five years I was made a partner in the firm, but I was already beginning to feel a lack of challenge with accountancy, and I felt that my job was becoming too routine; accountancy in those days was not nearly as varied and rewarding as it is now. As part of my job,

David's office is over Dutton-Forshaw's garage in Lytham St Annes, about half-an-hour's drive from Preston.

I used to do regular audits for Loxhams Garages (as it was called before it was taken over by the Dutton-Forshaw Motor Group), and over the years I gradually developed an interest in the motor trade. Just before the company was taken over, I was completing an audit when the then managing director invited me to work for him as a group secretary, to handle the administration and accounting side of the company's affairs.

Because of my growing interest in the trade, which I thought was more exciting and held better career prospects than accounting, I accepted. As well as a higher salary and a company car, I found my new job to be particularly challenging.

Since then, my career has followed a steady pattern of promotion within the company. After the take-over by Dutton-Forshaw, I served for five years as secretary for the North West region. When the managing director was put in charge of the company's operations in the whole of the north of England, I was promoted to regional managing director in Merseyside. For two years after that I did the same job in the larger North East region, until six years ago, when I was given my present post as regional managing director for the North West. In 1980, my region was expanded to include Merseyside, so I now have a large area to look after.

As far as Dutton-Forshaw is concerned, the main criterion of success in my job is the production of profit. The most important qualities you need to have in my job are plain commonsense, and the basic ability to understand and motivate other people, because my position is one of leadership in a very large team – in my region I have 350 people working under me. The most useful thing I have ever learnt is my basic accounting training, because it taught me the simple, but essential lesson of the necessity to keep income up and expenses down.

In line with most prudent motor distributors, as part of our cost-cutting procedures we've reduced our levels of manpower in the last six years. Before then, we used to employ as many as 1,000 people in this region alone, but various factors have forced us to cut back our numbers of branches and employees. The greatest single factor has been the growth in sales of imported cars, for which we don't have a franchise – 55 per cent of all cars sold in this country are made abroad. But the drop in sales during the recession, higher wage levels, and improvements in car design, which mean that cars don't have to be serviced so often, have all contributed to our reduction in manpower. Now that we have cut back our number of branches in line with the BL franchise plan, we are gearing up to take advantage of the tremendous market awaiting the new products of the company.

The main responsibilities in my job are, firstly, to produce a profit; to keep control of stocks and other assets; and to satisfy the customers in my region. Without satisfied customers, there is no business. I also have to motivate my staff, and keep them interested in their jobs.

My work is not the sort which you can leave and forget about at 5.00 p.m. It tends to take up most of my life, and there is no such thing as a typical routine day. Sometimes I literally work from dawn to dusk, arriving at the office at 8.00 a.m. and leaving well after 7.30 p.m. After that I might have to attend a special promotion evening in one of our showrooms, or go to a business dinner, which can last until 10.00 p.m. On Saturday mornings, and for a couple of hours each Sunday, I work in my office, and I usually have paperwork to do at home. I used to be a keen sportsman, playing rugby and cricket, but as you can imagine, I rarely have the time these days, even as a spectator. The only time I can really relax is

In his office he sorts out the post with his secretary.

David regularly visits the Dutton-Forshaw garage.

He takes a look at work going on in the main workshops at the Preston garage.

when I take my family on holiday to our favourite resort in Spain, and I really look forward to these breaks. Sometimes I also go abroad for product launches or trade conferences, but these trips are sponsored by manufacturers and suppliers, and are very much part of my job.

My office is at Lytham St Annes, about half-an-hour's drive from Preston, and my first job in the morning is to open my mail and deal with any correspondence. I then spend an hour or so telephoning our branches, customers, or suppliers, sorting out any problems which may have arisen. Until lunchtime, the next couple of hours are usually taken up with writing reports of various kinds, concerning, for example, the proposed aquisition of a new business, or monthly trading figures. I give these to my secretary for typing, and go for a working lunch, perhaps with a supplier, or one of my branch managers.

After lunch I usually visit one of our branches to go through the accounts and sort out any practical problems – I regularly make these visits to all my branches. I'm usually back in the office by 5.00 p.m. to sign the letters which my secretary has typed, before making more telephone calls. An hour later, I may have a meeting with the head office staff to review the day's business and make any necessary decisions about the company's affairs in the region. If I'm lucky, before going home I have a well-earned pint of beer in a local pub, but as soon as I walk in, someone always starts talking to me about motor cars!

As well as being responsible for this region, I'm also involved in the company's affairs on a national level. I report to the group managing director for the whole country. I'm in constant contact with him, and I send him a written report once a month. The group executive committee also meets once a month to discuss Dutton-Forshaw's national issues and policies.

Just about the only thing I don't enjoy about my job is making people redundant, but sometimes this is necessary to streamline the company, and keep its position as a healthy and efficient business. A lot of people don't like the paperwork which their job entails, but I don't really mind it at all. I make sure that I run the paperwork, rather than it running me, and I find that I can get through it quite quickly.

I very much enjoy my job – apart from my family, it is my life. The work is very varied, and I never have a dull moment because there is always something different happening. I enjoy being busy, which is fortunate in my job! I also feel that the motor trade is an important one; as well as employing thousands of people in this country, a motor car is an important object in everyone's life. For most people, it is the second largest purchase they are likely to make in their life, after their house.

To a certain extent, my pay depends on the profit we make in our region – the more successful I am in my job, the more I earn. The company also provides me with certain benefits, or 'perks', as part of the rewards for my work. I have a Jaguar company car, I can reclaim expenses for business lunches, I have free BUPA medical cover, free life assurance, and permanent sickness benefit, should I be taken ill.

David studies the stock situation of cars in the Preston garage office.

I feel that it should be everyone's ambition to climb higher in their careers. Ambition is an important quality in anyone, no matter how high they have risen already, and no-one should be content to sit back and accept that they can go no further.

David and his staff examine a new Rolls-Royce.

Appendices

Jobs in a garage

Management staff
Managing director
General manager
Personnel manager
Service manager
Parts manager
Training manager
Forecourt manager
Sales manager
Car-hire manager
Accountant
Computer analysts and programmers

Productive staff
Car salesmen
Fleet salesmen
Mechanics
Electricians
Trimmers
Panel beaters
Painters
Parts sales staff
Parts representatives

Finance department staff
Contract hire clerks (for fleets)
Leasing clerks
Hire purchase clerks
Insurance department clerks

Supervisory staff
Foremen
Service receptionists
Parts supervisors
Workshop controllers

Support staff
Van drivers
Cleaners
Forecourt attendants
Clerical workers
Car-hire clerks
Maintenance men
Cashiers
Computer operators

Sources of further information

Motor Agents Association
201 Great Portland Street
London W1N 6AB

Scottish Motor Trade Association
3 Palmerston Place
Edinburgh EH12 5AQ

Institute of the Motor Industry
Fanshaw's
Brickendon
Hertford SG13 8PQ

Society of Motor Manufacturers and Traders
Forbes House
Halkin Street
London SW1X 7DS

Road Transport Industry Training Board
Capitol House
Empire Way
London HA9 0NG

City and Guilds of London Institute
46 Britannia Street
London WC1X 9RG

Some useful books are:

A BP Garage by Paul Moody (Wayland 1982)
Cars by Christopher Pick (Gallery Press 1979)
In a Garage by John Dyson (Wayland 1975)
Motor Cars by Cyril Posthumus (Wayland 1982)
Working with Cars by John Moorey (Batsford 1981)

Index

A

Amalgamated Union of Engineering Workers 14
ambitions and prospects 28, 29, 33, 43, 48, 53, 55, 62, 67
  lack of 14, 19, 38
applications for jobs 10, 15, 21, 24, 29, 34, 39, 54
Army 34, 63

B

Blackburn Technical College 16
Blackpool and Fylde College of Further Education 36
Blackpool Technical College 26
bodyshop 8, 24–8
Bolton Institute of Technology 58

C

canteen/restroom 18, 26, 32, 37
car distribution system 6
Certificate of Secondary Education 10, 15, 24, 34, 39, 44
City and Guilds course in body repairing 26
City and Guilds course in mechanics 31
City and Guilds course in painting and trimming 36
City and Guilds Technological Certificate 39
clocking on 18, 26, 31, 47
colleges
  Blackburn Technical College 16
  Blackpool and Fylde College of Further Education 36
  Blackpool Technical College 26
  Bolton Institute of Technology 58
  Tuson College, Preston 16, 44
computers 15, 17, 45, 47, 60, 61
cost accounting 44–8
customer relations 18, 19, 54–7

D

day-release 11, 16, 26, 36, 39
departments in Dutton-Forshaw, Preston
  bodyshop 8, 24–8
  cost accounting 44–8
  delivery service 20–23
  parts store 15–19
  Rolls-Royce section 39–43
  sales 58–62
  service and repair workshop 8, 10–14
  sprayshop 26
  trimming/upholstery 34–8
Diploma in Business Studies 44
Diploma of the Institute of Marketing 58
Dutton-Forshaw Motor Group 7, 8, 64
  Preston branch 8, 9
  Lytham St Annes branch 66

E

educational qualifications
  CSE 10, 15, 24, 34, 39, 44
  Diploma in Business Studies 44
  GCE 'A' level 36, 58, 63
  GCE 'O' level 10, 20, 24, 34, 39, 44, 58, 63
  Higher National Diploma in Business Studies 58
employment opportunities in a garage 6, 7
equipment 12, 27, 28, 33, 42
evening classes 19, 36, 48, 49

F

first impressions of work 16, 22, 24, 33, 35, 45, 59
Ford, Henry 6
  'Model T' 6
forecourts 6
franchise
  with BL 8, 60, 65
  with Rolls-Royce 8, 60

G

General Certificate of Education 10, 20, 24, 34, 36, 39, 44, 58, 63

H

Higher National Diploma in Business Studies 58
hobbies and interests 14, 19, 23, 32, 33, 43, 48, 52, 57, 62
holidays 14, 33, 48, 57, 62, 66

I

interviews 10, 15, 21, 24, 29, 30, 34, 39, 50, 54, 58
  qualities looked for by interviewers 52, 61
Institute of Marketing, Diploma 58
Institute of the Motor Industry 39
  management course 16

J

jobcentres 10, 20

K

Kirkham Grammar School 63

L

Leycare scheme 11, 12, 14
Loxhams Garages 8, 64

M

Manpower Services Commission 29
Ministry of Transport 11
MOT certificates 11, 12

Motor Agents Association 6
motor trade 6, 7
Motor Vehicle Technician's course 39

N

National Craftsmen's Certificate 39
National Joint Council of the Motor Vehicle Industry 19, 28
Navy 34
numbers employed in garages 6

O

Opinions of jobs 14, 19, 21, 28, 36, 38, 43, 48, 53, 57, 62, 67

P

parts store 15–19
pay 14, 19, 28, 33, 38, 43, 48, 67
professional institutions
  Institute of the Motor Industry 39
  Motor Agents Association 6
professional qualifications
  City and Guilds course in body repairing 26
  City and Guilds course in mechanics 31
  City and Guilds course in painting and trimming 36
  City and Guilds Technological Certificate 39
  Motor Vehicle Technician's course 39
  Service Reception Certificate 39

R

RAF 34, 54, 55
Rolls-Royce section 39–43

S

safety at work 28, 33
sales department 58–62
schools
  Kirkham Grammar School 63
  William Temple High School 24
service and repair workshop 8, 10–14
Skills Assessment Test 26
social and sports club 53, 62
spare-time work 23, 33, 48
sprayshop 26
staff discounts and benefits 19, 23, 43, 53, 57, 67

T

trade unions 14, 27, 36, 41
training courses 11, 12, 26, 41, 51, 55, 59
training school 30
trimming/upholstery department 34–8
Tuson College, Preston 16, 44

W

William Temple High School 24
working hours 12, 18, 22, 26, 31, 37, 41, 47, 51, 56, 65

Y

Youth Opportunities Programme 44, 45
Youth Training Scheme 7–9, 29–33, 45